The

GREAT
GOLF COURSES
OF CANADA

Revised and Updated

The
GREAT GOLF COURSES OF CANADA

Revised and Updated

by John Gordon
Photography by Michael French

FIREFLY BOOKS

A Firefly Book

Published by Firefly Books Ltd. 1999

Third Edition, First Printing

Library of Congress Cataloging-in-Publication Data

Gordon, John.
    The great golf courses of Canada: third edition / by John Gordon ; photography by Michael French.
[240] p. : col. ill. ; cm.
Summary : Detailed course descriptions, accurate aerial maps, short features and over 200 photographs of 38 golf courses in Canada.
ISBN 1-55209-341-7
1. Golf courses – Canada – Directories.   I. French, Michael, ill.
II. Title.
796.352 – dc21   1999   CIP

Canadian Cataloguing in Publication Data

Gordon, John (John William)
    The great golf courses of Canada

3rd ed.
ISBN 1-55209-341-7

1. Golf courses – Canada. I. Title.

GV985.C35G725 1999   796.352'06'871   C98-932731-0

Published in Canada in 1999 by
Firefly Books Ltd.
3680 Victoria Park Avenue
Willowdale, Ontario, Canada
M2H 3K1

Published in the United States in 1999 by
Firefly Books (U.S.) Inc.
P.O. Box 1338, Ellicott Station
Buffalo, New York, USA
14205

Produced for Firefly Books Ltd. by Warwick Publishing Inc.,
a division of the Warwick Communications Group.
Front cover photograph: Grey Wolf

Printed and bound in Canada by Friesens, Altona, Manitoba

To Leslie

ACKNOWLEDGEMENTS

Listing acknowledgements is a no-win situation, because you are bound to leave someone off the list. To that someone, or several someones, I apologize. Having said that, there are also some anonymous someones, whose names I will never know, who deserve a nod of appreciation. Those are the people who produce the yardage guides, brochures, scorecards and other materials that bulge my files at present and that helped immeasurably during the assembly of this book.

Among individuals, I would single out Nick Pitt, my long-suffering publisher at Warwick Communications. Without his unique blend of patience, humour and direction, this book would not have been published.

And even the most egomaniacal ink-stained wretch would be hard pressed to deny the impact of the fabulous photographs of my longtime collaborator Michael French.

Other contributors who deserve mention include architects Thomas McBroom (and, especially, the incomparable Mary Thring of his staff), Doug Carrick, Michael Hurdzan and Ron Garl.

Life was also made easier for the author by Kevin Thistle (Angus Glen); Sandy Campbell, Scott Macaulay, Irene Khattar and Joe Robinson (Bell Bay and Highlands Links); Ed McLaughlin (Big Sky and Nicklaus North); Murray Blair (Chateau Whistler); John Wilson (Heritage Pointe); Franz Hasenhundl (Mont Tremblant); Chris Goodwin (Redtail); Dawn Pentesco and Doug Ball (Devil's Pulpit Golf Association); Jim McLaughlin (Westwood Plateau).

Special thanks to Vivian Cadieux for holding down the fort; Dan and Hazel St. Amand for their island hospitality; and Marc Rochette, for being as good a photographer as he is a friend.

Most of all to Clan Gordon: Leslie, Will, Allie and Maggie. You know why.

TABLE OF CONTENTS

INTRODUCTION

Eight years ago, I wrote in the introduction to the first edition of *The Great Golf Courses of Canada* that "Canada is blessed with exceptional golf courses from coast to coast, and that identifying your favourite layout is as subjective as choosing your spouse."

In the intervening years, those statements have become even more true.

Canada, like the rest of the world, continues in the heady rush of a golf course construction boom seldom before witnessed. Only the fervour of the early 1920s exceeded what has happened in this country in the past decade. You need look no further for evidence than the book you are holding in your hands.

In the first edition, we selected 38 of the best courses in Canada. Not *the* best. Some of the best. It was a difficult challenge, to say the least. Most of the selections were historic clubs, scattered from Vancouver Island to Newfoundland. When edition two was published in 1993, we included some notable newcomers, but retained a core of the older courses for balance.

Now, in this, the third edition, we were presented with an array of tremendous new contenders. The choices were difficult, but we think we made the right ones. The thoroughbreds in this edition are a mix of old and new, classic and modern. The balance reflects the fabulous, and largely unacknowledged, breadth of golf experiences available among Canada's 2,000 courses.

Enjoy.

John Gordon
January 1999

*Every hole at Banff features the
natural beauty of the Rockies.*

BANFF SPRINGS

Golf Course

*Architects: Stanley Thompson (18)
Bill Robinson (9)
Head Professional: Doug Wood
Manager: Stan Bishop
Superintendent: Bernie Thiesen*

Banff Springs, it is said, was the first golf course to cost $1 million to build. The original 18 holes represented a test of man using machinery to mould nature to his purposes rather than fighting it into submission. "Nature must always be the architect's model," said course designer Stanley Thompson. Despite those sentiments, there was no avoiding the fact the thousands of tons of rock had to be blasted and hundreds of trees had to be sacrificed to create this masterpiece which came into being in 1927. So skilful was this act of creation that, in maturity, the course appears one with nature.

Those 18 holes now are labelled the Rundle and Sulphur nines, while another nine, Tunnel, was designed by Bill Robinson of British Columbia and put into play in 1989. "We tried to make it as similar to the old course as we could," Robinson said. The three nines are played in various combinations, but it is the original 18 of which golfers speak with reverence. The setting is unparalleled. In the shadow of Mount Rundle, Sulphur Mountain and Tunnel Mountain, the holes stretch along the Bow River within the confines of Banff National Park. The beauty of the course and the surrounding terrain are breathtaking: pine forests, crystal-clear water, snowy

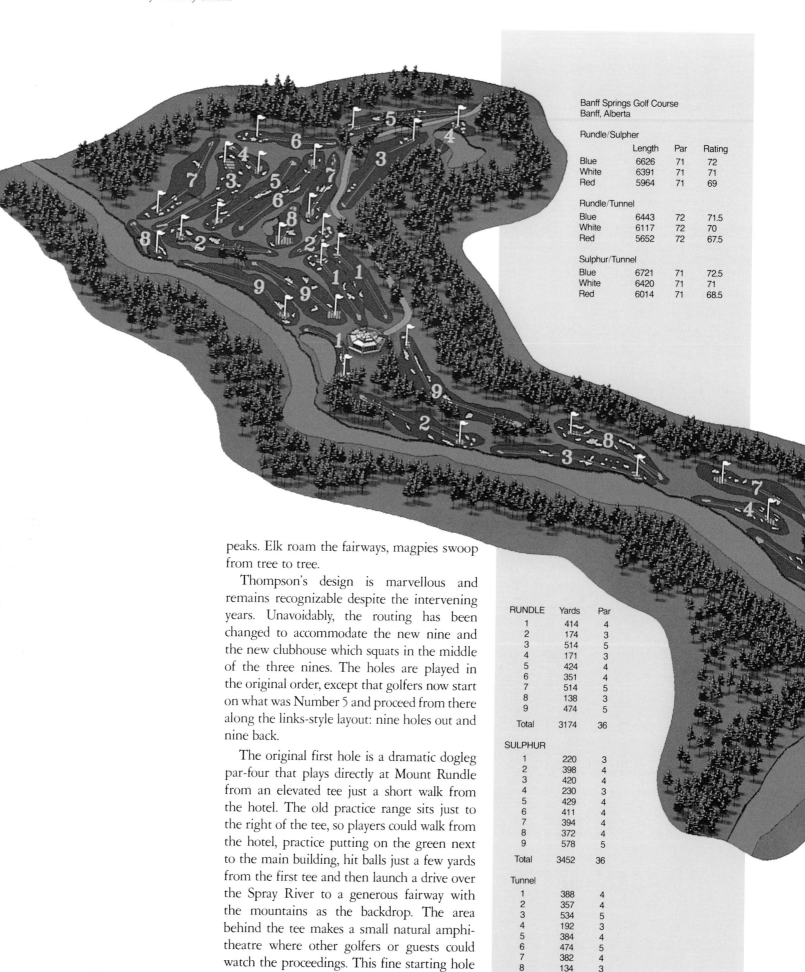

Banff Springs Golf Course
Banff, Alberta

Rundle/Sulpher

	Length	Par	Rating
Blue	6626	71	72
White	6391	71	71
Red	5964	71	69

Rundle/Tunnel

	Length	Par	Rating
Blue	6443	72	71.5
White	6117	72	70
Red	5652	72	67.5

Sulphur/Tunnel

	Length	Par	Rating
Blue	6721	71	72.5
White	6420	71	71
Red	6014	71	68.5

peaks. Elk roam the fairways, magpies swoop from tree to tree.

Thompson's design is marvellous and remains recognizable despite the intervening years. Unavoidably, the routing has been changed to accommodate the new nine and the new clubhouse which squats in the middle of the three nines. The holes are played in the original order, except that golfers now start on what was Number 5 and proceed from there along the links-style layout: nine holes out and nine back.

The original first hole is a dramatic dogleg par-four that plays directly at Mount Rundle from an elevated tee just a short walk from the hotel. The old practice range sits just to the right of the tee, so players could walk from the hotel, practice putting on the green next to the main building, hit balls just a few yards from the first tee and then launch a drive over the Spray River to a generous fairway with the mountains as the backdrop. The area behind the tee makes a small natural amphitheatre where other golfers or guests could watch the proceedings. This fine starting hole now is the 15th.

The former finishing hole (now the 14th,

RUNDLE	Yards	Par
1	414	4
2	174	3
3	514	5
4	171	3
5	424	4
6	351	4
7	514	5
8	138	3
9	474	5
Total	3174	36

SULPHUR		
1	220	3
2	398	4
3	420	4
4	230	3
5	429	4
6	411	4
7	394	4
8	372	4
9	578	5
Total	3452	36

Tunnel		
1	388	4
2	357	4
3	534	5
4	192	3
5	384	4
6	474	5
7	382	4
8	134	3
9	424	4
Total	3268	36

or the fifth of the Sulphur nine) is a strong dogleg par-four measuring 429 yards from the blues with more than two dozen bunkers all told. Some of these bunkers protect the driving area, some threaten faulty approaches, where others guard three sides of the green. The hole plays into the prevailing wind, so the second shot must often be a fairway wood or long-iron. The magnificent presence of the Banff Springs Hotel looms in the distance: a perfect home hole. With the new arrangement, the finishing hole is the old Number 4, a par-five, and no slouch at 580 yards from the blues with plenty of bunkers, mounds and swales.

The fairways at Banff Springs feature many sweeping contours to make drives and second shots challenging. Many fairways are bordered by mounds that tend to bring off-line drives back into play. Driving areas are moderately wide in most places, but the smart golfer will try to play to a particular location in the fairway to set up a favorable angle to the green. The contouring of the fairways and greens echoes the meandering movement of the Bow River and the surrounding terrain at the base of the mountains.

Most greens are canted toward the approaching golfer to receive incoming shots and many are raised above the level of the fairway. The golfer usually has the option of rolling the ball onto the greens; often the sole approach method for high-handicappers. The greens are not large by modern standards, although their size varies appropriately according to the shot the golfer is expected to play. They have many subtle contours and breaks that make three-footers treacherous, but they are not gimmicky.

The most memorable feature of Banff Springs is the bunkering. Most of the bunkers are located in or on mounds, and they feature flashed faces to make them visible from afar. As one approaches them, they change their shape and appearance, revealing new facets from different angles, just as the appearance of the surrounding mountains changes when seen from different angles or in different light.

Mis-hit approach shots tend to migrate into greenside bunkers, and certain key fairways bunkers also seem to attract off-line balls. Many fairway bunkers serve to catch errant shots and save them from the woods, while others indicate the preferred line: drive over them safely

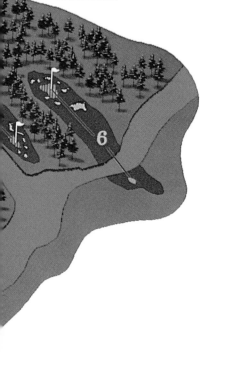

The "Little Bow" — another of Thompson's inspired par-threes.

The famed "Cauldron" at Banff Springs plays 171 yards over a mountain lake.

and you have a good angle for approaching the green. The bunkers are contoured such that the ball tends to roll down the face; one is never confronted with an "impossible" bunker shot.

The most exciting single shot is probably the tee shot at Number 4, the "Devil's Cauldron". The tee is quite elevated compared to the sloping green that is carved into the hillside about 170 yards away. The shot must carry over a glacial lake to the green, a shelf about 15 feet above the water level. Mount Rundle watches on the right. Club selection is tricky here: on a calm day, a smooth eight-iron; in the wind, use your imagination.

Banff's high elevation, more than 1,600 metres above sea level, means that the ball flies farther, perhaps one-to-two clubs' differ-ence. On the other hand, the wind varies from imperceptible to gale-force, meaning that downwind par-fours in excess of 400 yards can be played driver-wedge. As well, the mountain backdrops tend to distort one's perspective, making the business of judging distances a memorable experience, to say the least. The story is told of Gene Sarazen who ignored the advice of his local caddie, chose a club on his own, and barely made it halfway to the green.

The century-old Banff Springs Hotel, with more than 800 rooms, is a massive edifice that looks like a noble's castle in the Alps. The lobby and parts of the mezzanine are dark with heavy furniture; in places, it looks like a medieval fortress. The "new" addition was built in the 1920s and has recently received multi-million-dollar renovations.

Stanley Thompson was a genius at designing par-threes. Here, the 138-yard "Papoose."

Stanley Thompson (1894-1952)

Stanley Thompson was one of five brothers, all of whom achieved notoriety in golfing circles. Brothers Frank and Bill won the Canadian Amateur, Nicol was the head professional at Hamilton Golf and Country Club and Matt was a pro in Western Canada. Stanley, while a formidable player (he claimed the medalist title in the 1923 Canadian Amateur qualifying with a set of borrowed clubs), would become recognized as the dean of Canadian golf course architects. His memorials range literally from one coast of Canada to the other, from Capilano in West Vancouver to Highlands Links on Cape Breton Island. In between, he created masterpieces such as Jasper Park, Westmount, St. George's and a multitude of others. Banff, one of his crowning achievements, has the dubious distinction of being the first course in the world to cost more than $1 million to build. Thompson was one of three founders of the American Society of Golf Course Architects. The others were Donald Ross and Robert Trent Jones, at one time Thompson's junior partner.

Heritage Pointe, south of Calgary, boasts three superbly conditioned nines. The Pointe nine is routed through the rolling foothills of the Rocky Mountains. Here, the par-3 ninth hole and its tremendous green setting.

HERITAGE POINTE

Golf and Country Club

Semi-Private

Architect Ron Garl prefers the Gators college football team in his home state of Florida to the Calgary Stampeders of the Canadian Football League, and Heaven knows this Southern gentleman can't even imagine an Alberta winter, so just how did he end up designing the acclaimed Heritage Pointe Golf and Country Club just a few minutes south of Calgary?

"It's a long and unlikely story," drawls the loquacious and likable Garl. "I bumped into [Canadian golf professional] Alan Chud when I was doing some renovation work at Maple Downs in Ontario. One thing led to another and Alan and I ended up doing Heritage Pointe together."

Garl has designed layouts from Thailand to Costa Rica, but Heritage Pointe is his sole jewel north of the 49th Parallel. "We tried to schedule all our site visits for the summer," he confides.

"I did a lot of research into course design and construction," recalls Chud, who oversaw Heritage Pointe's evolution. "I

The Heritage nine at Heritage Pointe has been described as "a roller coaster ride of sheer delight." This is the par-3 third hole.

liked Ron's work and that aspect of the business really intrigued me."

The two worked unceasingly until the course opened in 1992, with Chud acting as Garl's site manager, and even designing a few holes himself. The result was impressive enough to vault the course to 18th spot in *SCORE* magazine's Top 50 ranking of Canadian courses in 1994, the first year it was eligible. In addition, it has received rave reviews from just about everyone who has played it. That includes the Canadian Tour professionals who play the Telus Calgary Open on the Desert and Heritage courses.

"Heritage Pointe is a great player's course because you have to think your way around to score well," says member Bob Legros, a scratch handicap who won the Amateur Golfers Association of Canada national championship in 1996. "It's a target-style course, with firm, fast greens and you have to shape your shots off the tee."

Of the three nines, the Desert is the most remarkable considering what they started with. "The land was basically a field of oats," recalls Chud. "We created a

desert-style course that looks like Arizona, except the waste areas are defined by different types of grasses." Exactly 21 different grasses, according to Garl, who has a university degree in turfgrass and is a director of the Florida Turfgrass Association.

"High plains desert chaparral" is how Garl describes the upper nine holes. (Chaparral is dense, tangled brushwood.) "That nine is basically built below the natural grade, similar to what Pete Dye did at PGA West [in the California desert]. What we did was dig everything down, instead of piling dirt up."

In doing so, they created a true test for even the best players on the Canadian Tour. While the Tour players were complimentary about the layout and the course conditioning, they were less than enthralled with how challenging the Desert nine was. The Prairie wind is omnipresent at Heritage Pointe. For instance, the 214-yard, par-3 third hole was ranked the most difficult during the 1997 Calgary Open, because it demanded a precise tee shot through the wind to a

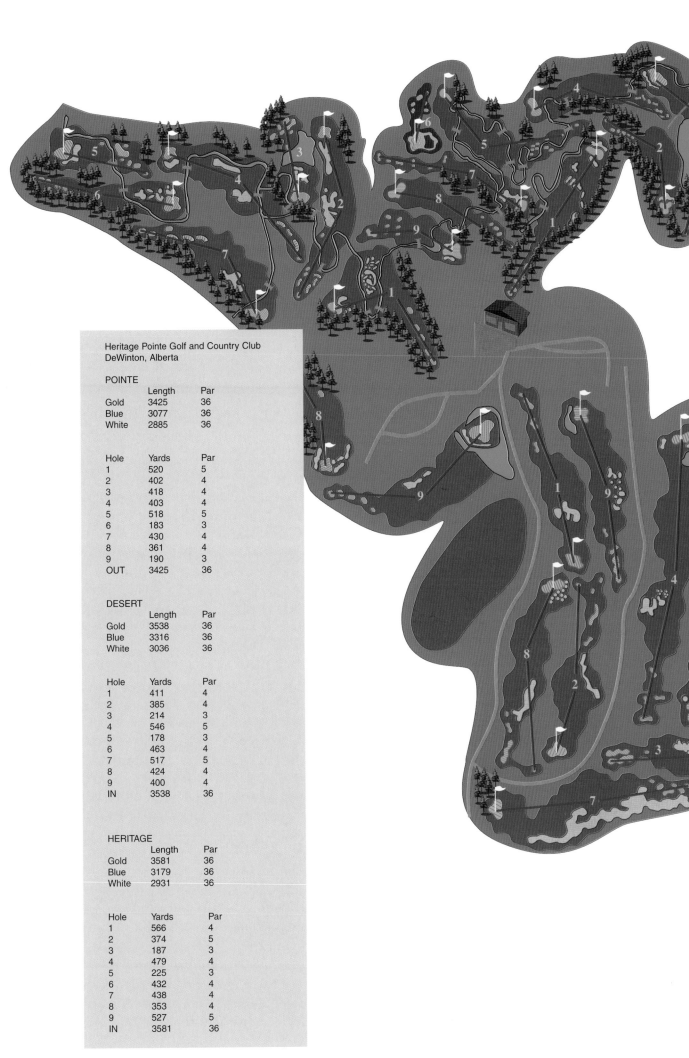

Heritage Pointe Golf and Country Club
DeWinton, Alberta

POINTE

	Length	Par
Gold	3425	36
Blue	3077	36
White	2885	36

Hole	Yards	Par
1	520	5
2	402	4
3	418	4
4	403	4
5	518	5
6	183	3
7	430	4
8	361	4
9	190	3
OUT	3425	36

DESERT

	Length	Par
Gold	3538	36
Blue	3316	36
White	3036	36

Hole	Yards	Par
1	411	4
2	385	4
3	214	3
4	546	5
5	178	3
6	463	4
7	517	5
8	424	4
9	400	4
IN	3538	36

HERITAGE

	Length	Par
Gold	3581	36
Blue	3179	36
White	2931	36

Hole	Yards	Par
1	566	4
2	374	5
3	187	3
4	479	4
5	225	3
6	432	4
7	438	4
8	353	4
9	527	5
IN	3581	36

An island green caps off the short but diabolical par-5 finishing hole of the Heritage nine.

well-bunkered green. The upwind 463-yard par-4 sixth hole, called Scotland, is reminiscent of traditional linksland, with its rolling fairway defined by tall, waving grasses and capacious bunkers.

The next hole, "Windswept," is a 517-yard par 5 that challenges the player not so much with length as with the daunting prospect of avoiding a waste bunker that runs 400 yards down the left side of the fairway. To complete the challenge, Windswept features a three-tiered green. The 424-yard eighth hole is aptly named "Deep Trouble" since it boasts no less than 12 pot bunkers, some of them 10 feet deep.

While John Wilson, director of golf operations, agrees that the Desert nine is unique, he emphasizes that the Heritage and Pointe nines are no weak sisters. "They are the most natural and most beautiful nines," he says, "and you get into lots of trouble with the tree-lined fairways, bunkers, and Pine Creek."

The Heritage nine has been described as "a roller coaster ride of sheer delight into the Pine Creek Valley." The tee shot on the 566-yard opening hole is hit some 200 feet down into the valley, creating a deceptively warm welcome for first-timers. A hard slap of reality comes soon enough, with three straight par 4s of more than 400 yards

capped off with "The Natural," a 518-yard dogleg bracketed by water and fescued mounds. Water comes into play on the Heritage nine several times, most notably surrounding the island green on the short but treacherous 497-yard par-5 ninth.

The Pointe nine, routed through the rolling foothills of the Rocky Mountains, begins with a breathtaking descent into the Pine Creek Valley. The delicious 520-yard, par-5 first hole sets the tone for a round that offers scenery but demands shotmaking. As Wilson points out, Pine Creek crisscrosses the par-5 fifth hole no less than five times (how appropriate).

The three possible 18-hole combinations play as long as 7,000 yards or as short as 4,700, and it is vital to select the tees appropriate for your skill level. "Every hole is different but each one is playable for all handicap levels from one of the four tee decks," Wilson says. "While only the really good players will post a low score, there is definitely a friendly side to Heritage Pointe."

Although his objectivity is questionable, Wilson describes Heritage Pointe as the "premiere public-access course in Western Canada and the best conditioned course, public or private, bar none."

Heritage Pointe: The first hole of the Heritage nine at Heritage Pointe can create a false sense of security, tempting you to blast a drive out into the abyss that drops some 200 feet down into Pine Creek Valley. Put discretion before valour, however, and choose a long iron or fairway wood to lay up short of the hazards. The second shot should trace the right side of the fairway on this par 5 in order to ensure the greenside bunkers do not intrude on the third shot.

The 520-yard opening hole of the Pointe nine at Heritage Pointe offers a breathtaking tee shot down into Pine Creek Valley.

*The dogleg 14th at Jasper Park
challenges the player to cut off as
much of the lake as he dares.*

JASPER PARK LODGE

Golf Course

*Architect: Stanley Thompson
Head Professional: Ron MacLeod
Manager: Perry Cooper
Superintendent: Brian Hill*

Jasper Park's classic 18-hole course was designed by Canada's greatest architect, Stanley Thompson, and opened for play in 1925. This splendid resort is located in Jasper National Park in the heart of the Rockies, just outside the town of Jasper on Lac Beauvert, where the water is green and clear. Nearby looms a range of rugged peaks called the Whistlers. The course winds through pine woods, affording golfers stunning views of the surrounding snow-capped mountains, which form a backdrop for most of the holes. Jasper Park's main challenges are the wind, the undulating fairways, the tricky greens and the fascinating bunkers.

The course sits close to the main lodge and some of the cabins. The practice range is 10 metres from the first tee and it is long enough for Greg Norman's longest drives. The holes move in an essentially circular pattern clockwise. Thus, the golfer's orientation with respect to the wind changes subtly from hole to hole; it is never really the same from one to the next. The course is a pleasant walk, with tees close by previous greens in all instances, and the elevation above sea level (about 1,000 metres) is not so extreme that one becomes winded because of the thin mountain air.

The holes are gently contoured with soft sweeping lines that

are most inviting and interesting to behold. Trees line both sides of many fairways, but landing areas are, for the most part, generous. Still, there are clearly preferred sides of the fairways if one hopes to have an advantageous line into the greens, which themselves tend to be medium-sized to smallish and set at angles to the fairways. They tend to be canted toward the approaching golfer and many are slightly elevated.

The front entrance to every green is open to allow running approach shots. Some greens, however, are raised enough that most successful approaches will fly all the way to the putting surface. The 16th green is guarded in front by water for more than three-quarters of its width; but a running shot to the extreme right side of the fairway could find the putting surface, if played to perfection.

The most notable feature of the course, after the spectacular setting, is Thompson's incomparable bunkering. His use of sand, here and at Banff Springs four hours to the south, could serve as a doctoral course in the fine art of

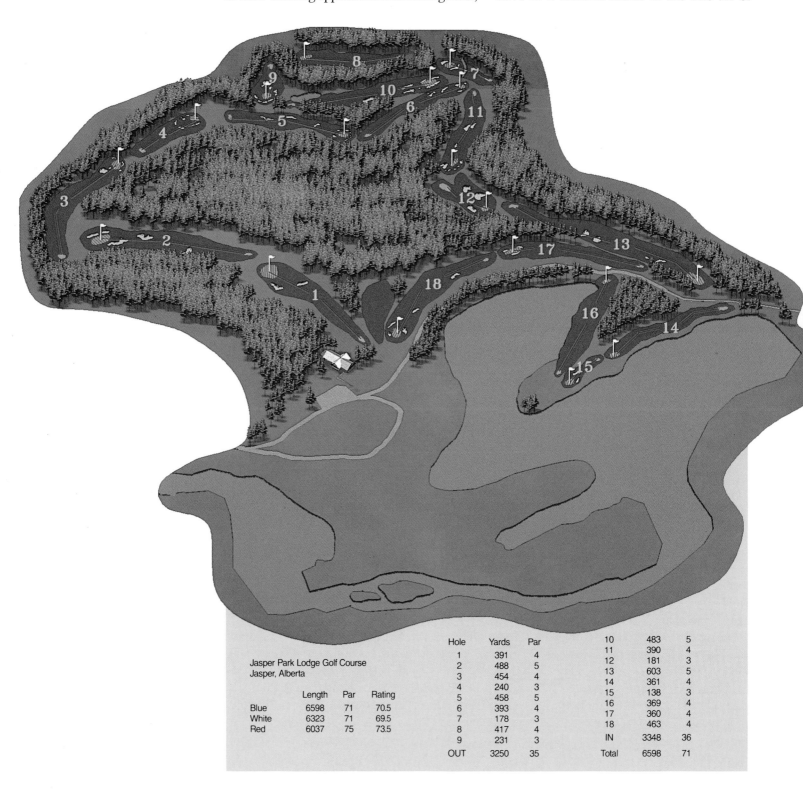

Hole	Yards	Par
1	391	4
2	488	5
3	454	4
4	240	3
5	458	5
6	393	4
7	178	3
8	417	4
9	231	3
OUT	3250	35

Hole	Yards	Par
10	483	5
11	390	4
12	181	3
13	603	5
14	361	4
15	138	3
16	369	4
17	360	4
18	463	4
IN	3348	36
Total	6598	71

Jasper Park Lodge Golf Course
Jasper, Alberta

	Length	Par	Rating
Blue	6598	71	70.5
White	6323	71	69.5
Red	6037	75	73.5

bunkering to frame fairways and greens, to provide interesting tactical and strategic challenges, and to enhance the beauty of an already gorgeous setting. The bunkers at Jasper Park are beautifully shaped and their appearance changes depending on the angle from which they are viewed. As you approach them, you see their appearance changing, just as you discover new facets in the surrounding mountains and the lake, every hour, every day.

Many of the bunkers are situated in or on mounds. Sand flashes up their faces so they can be seen from a distance. Some are substantial in depth, but they are gently graded so that errant shots usually finish up in a spot that allows a play toward the hole. Fairway bunkers indicate the line of play and, at some holes, save errant shots from the woods.

The greens are well protected at the sides and backs by bunkers that tend to gather mishit approaches. Several holes feature bunkers that guard the front of the greens but are perhaps 20 or 30 yards short of the actual putting surfaces. This arrangement puts a premium on club selection on approaches, especially as the flashed faces make it appear that the bunkers are tight to the greens. The greens have many subtle breaks and undulations, in addition to being steeply sloped from back to front in most cases.

The Jasper Park Lodge course is not particularly long, especially given the mountain setting, where the ball tends to carry farther than at sea level: 6,598 yards from the blues, 6,323 from the whites. Par is 71 as there are five par-threes. Thompson provided an excellent range of challenges for each kind of hole. Par-threes measure from 138 to 240 yards from the blues, from 120 to 220 from the whites; the par-fours include three in the 360-yard range and two at 454 and 468 respectively, from the blues. The par-fives range from a reachable 458 yards to a herculean 603. You will need every club in the bag here.

Many of the tees are elevated. The most exciting driving holes are Number 8, where you aim at a distant peak to try to place the ball between large mounds that guard both sides of the fairway; Number 14, a dogleg where the tee is situated on a small point and you cut off as much of the lake as you dare; Number 16 with its tight fairway guarded by water left

Greenside mounds at Jasper Park reflect the varying elevations of the distant mountain peaks.

Mountain streams and lakes join forces with Jasper Park's natural beauty to provide a scenic and sporting delight.

and trees right; and Number 18, a long, downhill dogleg with cavernous bunkers threatening every shot.

The 15th, called "The Bad Baby," is a superb par-three. It measures 138 yards from the blues, 120 from the whites, but it is a tantalizing target. The green is tiny, situated atop a mound with steep sides and a bunker left. Miss this green with your short-iron and you are assured of bogey or worse, especially if you have to pitch across the narrow putting surface. Thompson was unexcelled at designing par-threes.

The golf course is a gem and anyone with an interest in golf history or golf course architecture should find an opportunity to play this classic old course.

The accommodations at Jasper Park Lodge are on par with the course. The resort received the only gold medal awarded in Canada by the U.S. publication, GOLF, in 1989. The main lodge and surrounding cabins contain hundreds of rooms. The main building, built in the early 1950s, is beautiful, airy and peaceful. The floor is made of colorful flagstones; enormous picture windows look out to Lac Beauvert and the Whistlers; two huge fireplaces with hearths you could stand in are the focus of the sitting areas; massive beams and buttresses rise to the ceiling. The decor is tastefully done in every detail, both in the common areas and in the guest rooms. The cuisine and service are excellent and there is a myriad of activities for those few non-golfing hours.

In Love With Cleopatra

The single most memorable shot at Jasper Park Lodge is the tee shot at Number 9, "Cleopatra." A par-three that plays 231 yards from the blues, 214 from the whites, the tee is high on a hill, the green well below and heavily bunkered, sitting atop a mound with steep grassy sides. Choose your weapon, aim at a distant mountain top, and fire away: the drop from tee to green is so great that the ball seems to fly for minutes. The story is told that this hole derived its name as an offshoot of course architect Stanley Thompson's impish humor. Initially, as one stood on this tee, the voluptuous figure of Cleopatra became visible in the outlines of the fairway. Management of the Canadian National Railways, for whom Thompson built the course, persuaded him to disguise some of the contours, although the nickname stuck.

The appropriately named "Maze" is a short but convoluted par-five which starts off the back nine.

The mission at Kananaskis is to offer the green-fee player a private-club experience.

KANANASKIS

Country Golf Course

Architect: Robert Trent Jones
Director of Golf: Brian Bygrave
Head Professional: Wayne Bygrave
Superintendent: Jim O'Connor
Manager: Gord Sarkissian

No doubt, when Robert Trent Jones worked with revered Canadian course architect Stanley Thompson on his masterful layout at nearby Banff Springs, he dreamed of the time when he could tackle a similar challenge of his own in the awe-inspiring Rockies. He had to wait 50 years. His chance came in the early 1980s when the Alberta government decided to build a 72-hole golf facility in the Kananaskis River valley near Canmore, an hour west of Calgary.

The massive undertaking was funded by the Alberta Heritage Savings Trust Fund, staked by the province's huge oil production, and stands as a monument to both Jones and the foresight of the provincial government. Two courses, Mount Kidd and Mount Lorette, draw in the neighborhood of 75,000 golfers every season and it is safe to say that very few of that number are disappointed. They may echo Jones' sentiments when he first saw the proposed site: "the finest location I have ever seen for a golf course."

Despite their length — both layouts play to more than 7,000 yards from the tips — Jones provided four sets of tees to ensure that golfers of all abilities could enjoy his creations. Remember, as well, that the thin mountain air allows the ball to fly 10- to 15-per-cent further than at sea level; valuable input for club selection.

The par-three sixth hole on Mount Lorette — you will need a long-iron to a sharply sloping green protected by water.

All in all, Jones remained true to his design philosophy that each hole should be a tough par but an easy bogey.

Mount Kidd gives you little time to collect your wits before presenting what is rated the most difficult hole of its 18. The second hole is a par-five that stretches 536 yards from the white tees, usually into the wind. Take a moment on this tee to appreciate the green oasis that presents itself vividly against the grey granite backdrop of sheer mountain faces. Once back to reality, take care to avoid the righthand fairway bunkers with your tee shot and the river that edges up on the left as you approach the green. Four bunkers protect the relatively small green.

After negotiating the fourth hole, a par-three with a semi-island green that requires from a seven-iron to a four-iron with the wind at your back, you can start to anticipate the sixth. This challenging par-five is not overly long at 484 yards from the whites, but keeping the ball on the fairway is essential. The ideal landing spot is right, but that area is the location of a fairway bunker which complicates matters. A creek runs up the entire left side before looping behind the green and draining into a pond right of the putting surface. Dense forest guards the left boundary. The intelligent player will lay up in front of this tiered green.

Even taking the thin air into account, the finishing hole of Mount Kidd would make the longest hitters shudder. From the back tees, this hole is 642 yards, but the breathtaking scenery makes every moment spent here worthwhile. It has all the elements which characterize Kananaskis Country: dark-green forest, snow-capped mountains, shimmering water. Hit the tee shot as far as you can, bisect the fairway bunkers with a fairway wood on your second shot, place your mid- to short-iron approach on the right side of the pin, and you will be assured of a successful completion to your round.

Kananaskis Country Golf Course
Kananaskis Village, Alberta

Kidd	Length	Par	Rating
Gold	7049	72	74.5
Blue	6604	72	72
White	6068	72	69/74.5
Red	5539	72	66.5/71.5

Lorette	Length	Par	Rating
Gold	7102	72	74
Blue	6643	72	72
White	6155	72	69/76
Red	5429	72	64.5/72

Mount Kidd Course			Mount Lorette Course		
Hole	Yards	Par	Hole	Yards	Par
1	455	4	1	412	4
2	615	5	2	416	4
3	437	4	3	395	4
4	197	3	4	254	3
5	339	4	5	541	5
6	553	5	6	195	3
7	415	4	7	482	4
8	183	3	8	408	4
9	408	4	9	560	5
OUT	3602	36	OUT	3663	36
10	405	4	10	402	4
11	355	4	11	497	5
12	183	3	12	394	4
13	392	4	13	407	4
14	491	5	14	523	5
15	402	4	15	188	3
16	207	3	16	380	4
17	370	4	17	185	3
18	642	5	18	463	4
IN	3447	36	IN	3439	36
Total	7049	72	Total	7102	72

*Even facing as challenging a
hole as Mount Lorette's 17th, it
is almost impossible to ignore
the splendid surroundings.*

Moving on to Mount Lorette, you have a slightly more hospitable welcome than at Mount Kidd. The Number 1 rated hole doesn't appear until the fifth tee. At 478 yards, this par-five doesn't test the player's length, but accuracy is a must. A small creek cuts in front of the tee and continues through trees on the left before looping around and embracing the green on three sides. The tee shot must avoid the left fairway bunkers and the brave second shot, if going for the narrow kidney-shaped green in two, should be a faded fairway wood. Be wary of the hidden pond right of the green. Those less confident, or more sensible, should plan to lay up and hope for par.

Many players consider the seventh hole, a 439-yard par-four when played from the blues, the best on the course. Your drive must carry a large pond and stay out of fairway traps which litter the middle and left of the landing area. Being right of these is a mixed blessing because

the pond threatens that side. Those who are fortunate enough to avoid these hazards still must launch a long-iron into a well-bunkered, wavy green.

Touted as the most beautiful hole at Mount Lorette, the par-three 17th reminds the visitor why mountain golf in Canada is special. Lodge-pole pines direct your gaze at the mountains, and the Kananaskis River lies between tee and green, defined by three shimmering white sand traps.

The perfect outing at Kananaskis Country would be to play both courses in the same day, and it's not impossible because a round should not take longer than 4 1/2 hours. Golfers who complete 18 holes in less than that time are presented with a memento by the management. Kan-Alta Golf Management Ltd., which operates the facility under contract, promises to give public golfers a private-club experience and it's a credo they abide by.

*Designer Robert Trent Jones
called Kananaskis (opposite
page) "the finest location I have
ever seen for a golf course".*

———— *Ponoka, Alberta* ————

WOLF CREEK

Golf Resort

Architect: Rod Whitman
Director of Golf: Ryan Vold
Superintendent: Rick David
Manager: Randy Dool

Wolf Creek is where Canada meets Scotland. Not geographically, of course, but where else would you find a links-style course that uses bleached cattle skulls for 150-yard markers?

Credit Ryan Vold and Rod Whitman with the audacity to dream up Wolf Creek and the perseverance to see it come to fruition in 1984. Vold, a member of the Canadian Professional Golfers' Association, saw the potential for a unique golf course on a portion of his family's ranch south of Edmonton. Conveniently, his friend Whitman had apprenticed under famed U.S. course architect Pete Dye. Whitman surveyed the dunes covered with waving native grasses and wildflowers and visualized a tribute to the origins of golf, set in the Canadian West.

Links-style holes, complete with unmaintained rough and enormous waste bunkers, make up a large part of the Wolf's character. Other holes are lined with trees and provide a contrast to the undulating dunes. Although the scorecard reveals a total length of less than 6,600 yards from the tips, Wolf Creek ravages less-than-competent players who dare to play from the back tees. The scorecard advises that only those with a handicap of five or less should attempt the full length, while those who carry a handicap of 16 or higher should step up to the whites.

As the site of the Canadian Tour's Alberta Open, the course has been the recipient of some glowing reviews. Tour Commissioner Bob Beauchemin heads the list when he sums up what his players thought of the course: "To a man, every player has mentioned what a fair, intriguing, difficult, challenging, fun course it is to play. And there are very few courses where you get that kind of unanimous opinion." Prominent Tour player Matt Cole of Windsor, Ontario, concurs: "You can't get nonchalant over one shot — not one drive, not one iron, not one putt." And veteran Canadian pro Bob Panasik harks back to the history of the game, saying, "This is my conception of how golf started. It's a unique golf course in our country."

You get the full impact of that uniqueness

The semi-island green on No. 4 is a real challenge. A ball hit to the back of the island is almost impossible to stop.

from the time you drive into the parking lot. A 20,000-square-foot solid log clubhouse is hunkered down against the wind that sweeps across the Prairies and plays havoc with delicate approach shots.

Wolf Creek spares no mercy for those who do not come prepared to play. "If you can get through the first four or five holes," says Vold, "you've got it made. Number 2 and four kill more people in tournaments than you can believe."

The opening hole is a dogleg-right with spruce trees guarding the lefthand side and massive mounds defining the right. If you hit the landing area, an eight- or nine-iron should get you to the heavily undulating green. Like many approaches at Wolf Creek, this shot can be played two ways: a bump-and-run during

Designer Rod Whitman used Alberta's natural contours to produce remarkable holes such as the par-five 11th.

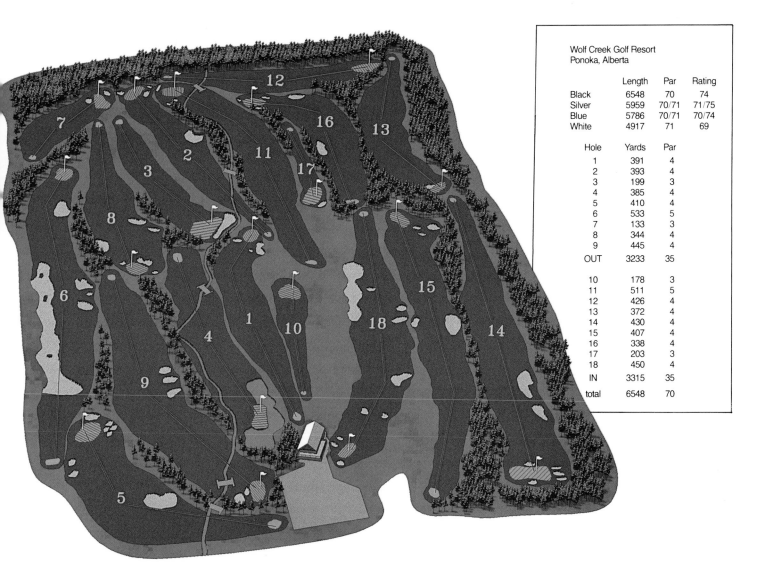

Wolf Creek Golf Resort
Ponoka, Alberta

	Length	Par	Rating
Black	6548	70	74
Silver	5959	70/71	71/75
Blue	5786	70/71	70/74
White	4917	71	69

Hole	Yards	Par
1	391	4
2	393	4
3	199	3
4	385	4
5	410	4
6	533	5
7	133	3
8	344	4
9	445	4
OUT	3233	35
10	178	3
11	511	5
12	426	4
13	372	4
14	430	4
15	407	4
16	338	4
17	203	3
18	450	4
IN	3315	35
total	6548	70

dry weather, or a high short-iron during wet spells.

On Number 2, you must negotiate your tee shot through a tree-lined chute to a landing area 230 yards out from the back tees. The two-tiered green is protected by a sod-walled bunker directly in front. The third hole is a 199-yard par-three that requires anything from a one- to a six-iron depending on the ever-present wind. A very natural hole, again, lined with spruces with a green that runs right to left.

From the elevated tees of Hawk's Alley, the par-four fourth hole, use a three- or four-wood to blast the ball between black spruces. Wolf Creek, the body of water, defines the left boundary of the hole before coming back into play in a most dramatic way: it surrounds the semi-island green. "This is a very severe green," says Vold. "Drop down one club on your approach and run the ball onto the green. If you fly it into the green and hit the downslope on the back level, you just might find yourself in the pond."

Don't think just because you've survived the first four or five holes that your work at Wolf Creek is done. Number 9 has claimed some good golfers and Vold calls holes 11 through 13 "our Amen Corner," referring to the tough holes at Augusta National, site of The Masters tournament.

Buffalo Jump, the par-five 11th hole, is a dogleg-left with a creek running in front of the green. If you are 210 yards or less to the green on your second shot, go for it. Otherwise, lay up and appreciate the naturalness of Whitman's characteristic "potato-chip" greens which flow right into the natural surrounding mounds.

Touring pro Brad King was leading the 1988 Alberta Open when he came to Number 12. When he stepped off the green, he had dropped entirely from the leaderboard after carding a 12. "Any hole at Wolf Creek can do that to you," says Vold. "You have to keep your focus all the way around. Don't fall asleep or it will grab you." The 12th is relatively unprepossessing; the dogleg-left simply requires that you stay out of the woods. Of course, there is a slight matter, hardly worth mentioning, of why they call this hole The Gorge. You must carry this ravine about 175 yards out to reach

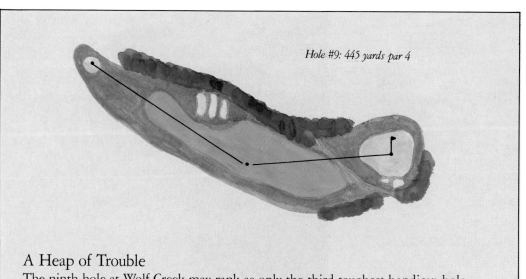

Hole #9: 445 yards par 4

A Heap of Trouble

The ninth hole at Wolf Creek may rank as only the third-toughest handicap hole on the course, but to at least a couple of Canadian Tour pros, there is no doubt it should be Number 1. During the 1990 Alberta Open, the 445-yard par-four claimed two victims in outrageous fashion. The hole calls for a long drive followed by a second shot over a ravine that features a creek and trees on either side. The green is not noted for being receptive to anything but a perfect approach. Toronto's Jack Kay Jr., a young pro with great talent who has played on the U.S. PGA Tour, thought he had it all together as he stepped onto the ninth tee. Twelve shots later, his ball collapsed with relief into the hole. One of Kay's compatriots, whose identity we are sworn not to reveal, took 14 whacks to complete this hole. He walked from the ninth green directly to his car, drove away and never looked back.

the landing area. Hit a fairway wood to the right side of the fairway.

The 13th hole completes this stretch. A drive to the upper deck on this dogleg-left leaves you only a short-iron into a flat green, half of which is hidden behind a steep-walled bunker.

Another nine holes, designed by Whitman in a similar, though even more natural, style were completed in 1990.

You must clear "The Gorge" on your way to parring the par-four 12th.

Architect Bob Cupp transformed a former potato field and a swamp into a glorious golf course ringed by mountains. Pictured is the par-4 seventh hole, swathed in early-morning mists.

BIG SKY

Golf and Country Club

Semi-Private

Big Sky Golf and Country Club sprawls across an alpine meadow at the foot of Mount Currie about 25 minutes north of the village of Whistler, or about two and a half hours from Vancouver. Although it is surrounded by British Columbia's Coast Mountain range, it is a flatland course, superimposed on a former potato farm. Its bentgrass tees, greens, and fairways are always in pristine condition and easy to walk.

Designed by Bob Cupp, whose other Canadian initiatives include Beacon Hall, Deerhurst Highlands, and Mad River in Ontario, Big Sky has four sets of tees, ranging from 7,001 yards to 5,208. As a result, it accommodates any calibre of golfer. It also tantalizes and rewards every player.

"When I looked at the land and the surrounding views, I thought, 'What we build here is going to be something special.' And, sure enough, Big Sky is everything we hoped it would be," Cupp says. What resulted from that potato farm

At 216 yards from the back tees, the 17th at Big Sky requires strength, accuracy, and some luck.

and swamp is indeed amazing. The designer used the open vistas to his advantage, creating a semi-links atmosphere, separating holes with mounding adorned with native grasses and wild flowers, rather than with stands of trees. The experience of playing Big Sky is capped off, logically enough, by the incredible views of the surrounding mountains.

"There are three significant disciplines in my design philosophy," Cupp says. "Strategic or tactical quality, the shot quality; esthetics; and conditioning. From a tactical point of view, tees have to be in the right place and the bunkers have to more acutely affect the player from the back tee than from the members' tee. And there are some places at Big Sky where the average player gets a tremendous advantage and other places where the average player has to execute what he or she may consider to be a heroic shot."

The par-5 fourth hole, 600 yards from the back tees, is a good example of Cupp's strategy. It heads straight toward the mountains, and the creek not only crosses the fairway no less than four times, it also runs laterally to the landing areas.

The tactical element places a premium on shot placement. If the tee shot is missed even slightly, it will require a heroic shot on the second. If the tee shot and the second shot are struck solidly, the ball may carry the third crossing of the creek. The hole requires everyone who plays it, regardless of their ability, to think on every shot. This hole is the entire Big Sky course in microcosm.

Cupp continues: "A lot of times, people are unaware why they play a certain hole well, but nine times out of ten it's because of their stance. That is something I really like to do, create stances. It is ultimately the most subtle thing you can do on a golf course.

"For instance, the consummate player playing off the back tees will be asked to hit the second shot from a hanging lie to a green sloped to accept a right-to-left shot. Everyone else will play into the green from a stance with the ball slightly above their feet which encourages a right-to-left shot. It's certainly a cranial game and worth all the effort you put into it."

In addition to a fine and varied quartet of par 3s, Cupp spiced up his design with

Big Sky Golf and Country Club
Pemberton, British Columbia

	Length	Par
Big Tees	7001	72
Blue	6496	72
White	6037	72

Hole	Yards	Par
1	450	4
2	413	4
3	194	3
4	600	5
5	161	3
6	349	4
7	380	4
8	393	4
9	536	5
OUT	3476	36
10	453	5
11	161	4
12	434	3
13	520	4
14	454	5
15	336	3
16	405	4
17	216	4
18	546	4
IN	3525	36
Total	7001	72

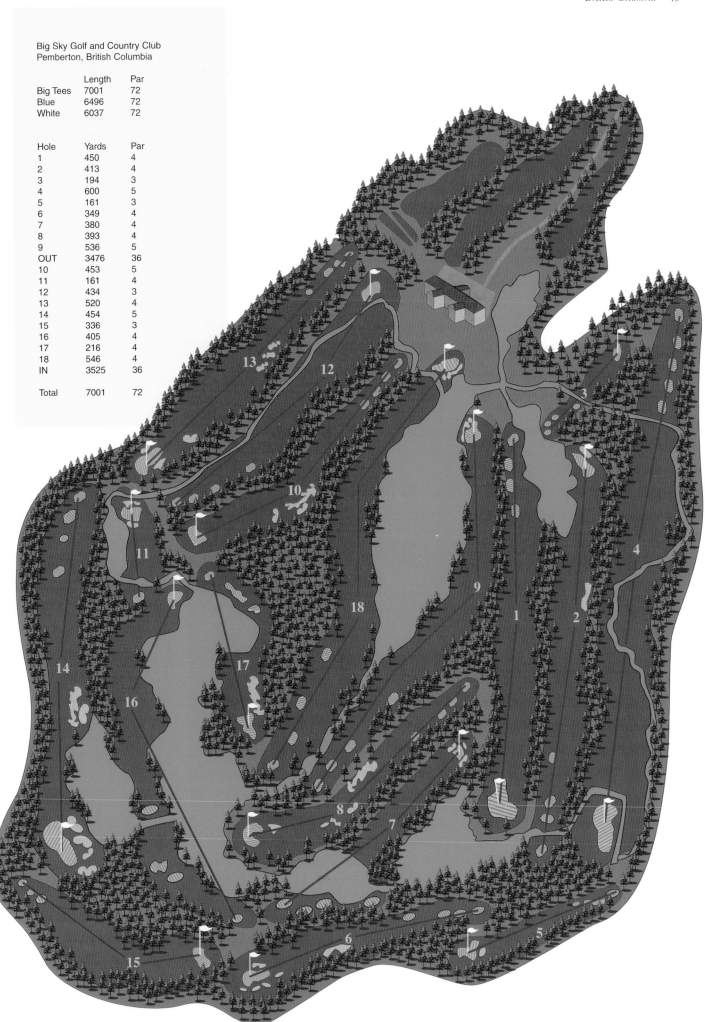

At only 336 yards from the championship tees, the par-4 15th hole at Big Sky is a dogleg left, suggesting the driver should remain in the bag.

solid par 4s. The long holes play into the prevailing wind, the short holes play downwind, bunker placements are strategic throughout, and greens range in size from tiny to enormous. At more than a few holes, improperly played approaches can bleed off into large, grassy swales. A clever chip is required to get close to the hole.

Among the finer par 4s are the 434-yard 12th, where the fairway is split by a creek; the 14th is a lengthy hole that parallels a dike constructed around the course to facilitate irrigation; and the 16th is a stellar two-shotter that bends from left to right around a lake, tempting players to bite off more than they can chew.

Big Sky is also characterized by the bordering Green River and seven lakes, all connected by meandering creeks. Though water skirts a dozen holes, playability is emphasized. According to Cupp's design associate, John Fought, "Anyone can make a course difficult. The trick is to create a course everyone can enjoy." Cupp and Fought have achieved that trick here. As a result, Big Sky received a platinum award from *Golf Course Ranking Magazine*, got a four-star rating in *Golf Digest*'s "Places To Play" publication, was named the 1998 B.C. Golf Facility of the Year, and was included in North America's top 100 list by *Golf For Women* magazine.

Big Sky also features a 350-yard, double-ended driving range, two practice holes with multiple tees, seven practice bunkers, and three putting greens. The Big Sky Golf Academy is renowned as one of the top teaching facilities in Western Canada. Big Sky also offers its Kaddyshack for kids aged three to twelve, which allows parents to play a round of golf secure in the knowledge that their children are being cared for by competent child-care workers.

Big Sky: (4th hole) Welcome to Purgatory. The top-ranked stroke hole at Big Sky is a full 600 yards from what the scorecard calls the "Big Tees." You tee off at the mountains and try to avoid a creek that traverses the fairway four times as well as hemming the landing areas. Better to play it smart on this monster, settling for a bogey, perhaps, but avoiding the downward descent from Purgatory to sheer hell! Another approach for the faint of heart (or sensible) is to play from the blue (520 yards), white (480), or red (448) tees.

The par-4 second hole is typical of the Big Sky experience. Although set in the mountains, it is relatively flat, more like a heathland course.

*Often called one of the world's
most scenic courses, Capilano sits
high above the port city of
Vancouver.*

————West Vancouver, British Columbia————

CAPILANO

Golf and Country Club

Architect: Stanley Thompson
Head Professional: Gerry Chatelain
General Manager: Rob Cowan

Understandably, many first-time visitors to Capilano find it hard to concentrate on playing one of Stanley Thompson's finest creations because they are so awed by its spectacular setting. Capilano Golf and Country Club, nestled in the mountains overlooking the beautiful harbor city of Vancouver, is no doubt the most scenic golf course in this country, and must be in the Top 10 in the world in that category. But those novices will soon realize that the demands the course makes on their visual senses will be equalled by the demands on their golfing abilities.

"Visually, it's a gorgeous course," says PGA Tour pro Jim Nelford, who grew up on the West Coast and who has played around the world. "The course is cut right out of the forest. It's away from the city, above the smog. When you get on the first tee, you get a view of all of Vancouver. You just look down the hill and the city is laid out in front of you. And then when you're through playing, it's a real pleasure to go into the clubhouse, which is a grand old thing that sits way on top of everything. You can see the last five holes from the clubhouse, as well as the first hole and the 13th green. What a breathtaking view from up there. Capilano is an old course with plenty of class. . . . One of the best courses I've ever played."

Capilano's very private enclave in the hills of West Vancouver offers a memorable golfing experience for pro or amateur.

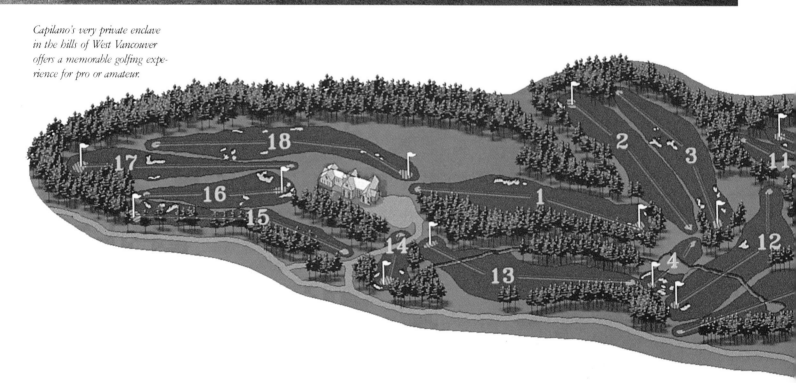

This unparalleled experience grew from the vision and determination of A.J.T. Taylor, an investment broker who was born on Vancouver Island in 1887, and is indelibly linked with the development of West Vancouver itself. Taylor negotiated the purchase of 6,000 acres (at $20 an acre) across the inlet from Vancouver, offering wealthy Britons a land development opportunity. The area, still known as the British Properties and one of the most prestigious locales in the region, at the time was linked with Vancouver only by slow, unreliable ferries. Taylor, using the financial clout of the Guinness Brewing Co., a major investor in the British Properties, bullied through the building of a bridge to the city. The Lions Gate Bridge cost $5.7 million and was the second-longest suspension bridge in the world at the time, trailing only San Francisco's Golden Gate Bridge.

Auspiciously, the bridge was opened by King George VI in 1939, the same year as the clubhouse at Capilano Golf and Country Club, the jewel in the British Properties crown. Seven years earlier, Taylor had enlisted the outstanding Canadian course architect Stanley Thompson to design a layout on Hollyburn Mountain west of the Capilano River. (Thompson received less than $7,000, including fees, plans and expenses, for his labors.)

"We feel hopeful that this project may prove our best endeavor on this continent," says Thompson in correspondence to the course developers. Considering Thompson's body of work, that was a tall, but prophetic, statement. That the course has remained largely unchanged from that original design is testimony to Thompson's abilities and a tribute to an intelligent membership with a continuing deep understanding of the game.

Jock McKinnon, who was the revered head professional here for 42 years, put it this way: "Capilano was and still is a tribute to the architectural genius of Stanley Thompson. There is no need for any tampering apart from taking care of the normal wear and tear. The members have a work of art in their care and possession. My advice is that they should never permit this to be spoiled by people who come along as they have done, and will, and suggest changes at great cost in what I think is a useless attempt to improve a great golf course."

Capilano has had an illustrious membership. In 1937, one year after the course opened, the country's top-ranked amateur arrived and and stayed to make an indelible impression on the club's stately and sensible development. Ken Black, then 26 years old, won the 1939 Canadian Amateur and was made one of the club's first honorary members. He did not play in another national championship until 1946 (the tournament was suspended during the war years) and, much like another famed amateur, Bobby Jones, retired from competitive golf prematurely. Only 34, he became very active in club affairs and is regarded as a guiding

Capilano Golf and Country Club
West Vancouver, British Columbia

	Length	Par	Rating
Blue	6578	72	72
White	6274	72	70
Yellow	5964	74	74

Hole	Yards	Par
1	482	5
2	400	4
3	467	5
4	172	3
5	520	5
6	394	4
7	426	4
8	381	4
9	176	3
OUT	3418	37
10	434	5
11	165	3
12	368	4
13	400	4
14	130	3
15	430	4
16	247	3
17	425	4
18	557	5
IN	3156	35
Total	6574	72

Towering evergreens line Capilano's fairways and make accuracy a must.

light. Other members have claimed national titles and Capilano has played host to innumerable tournaments at all levels.

The club has also been a gracious host to an international who's who, ranging from Bob Hope, Bing Crosby and Billy Graham, to heads of state such as the prime ministers of Japan and Malaysia. In 1971, the clubhouse was the site of a notable wedding reception, that of Pierre and Margaret Trudeau.

"Apart from its natural beauty, this is an ideal golf course," says former Masters champion George Archer, now a standout on the Seniors Tour, "because it is a fair test for the members from the middle tees, and is easily transformed into an excellent championship course from the back tees without tricking up the greens or the rough or the approaches."

To get the best from your round at Capilano, "get your birdies early," says Head Professional Gerry Chatelain. There are three reachable par-fives in the first five holes here, offering an opportunity to gain a couple of strokes from par. The test may come right after those five holes, on the relatively undemanding sixth hole. This short par-four, a drive and a wedge

for most players, has proved to be the most difficult hole in many of the tournaments played here, says Chatelain. To get your four, hit an iron off the tee into the narrow landing area; above all, don't miss the fairway.

Holes seven and eight also claim their share of victims. On the seventh, the Number 1 stroke hole at Capilano, a drive into a gully leaves you with any combination of uneven lies. From there, you hit through a very narrow entrance to a difficult green. Number 8 shares some characteristics with the preceding hole: a shortish par-four with a well-protected green, and a predilection for bogeys.

Once you reach the final four holes, you may regret not having heeded Chatelain's advice about concentrating on those early birdie chances. Capilano's strong finishing holes start at the dogleg-left, par-four 15th, which is followed by a 250-yard par-three. The 17th hole is another strong par-four. The final hole is a tough par-five that features a blind shot into the largest green on the golf course, meaning the emphasis is on correct club selection. The green is on a plateau and protected by bunkers.

Jock McKinnon's Eclectic Record

Jock McKinnon, Capilano's head pro for 42 years, was a fine player in his own right. He is in the record book, however, for a golfing feat that may never be equalled: an eclectic score of 33, recognized by the Guinness Book of World Records. An eclectic score is the sum of a player's all-time personal low scores for each hole on one course, and McKinnon's record is 33, accomplished over 21 years. His eclectic scorecard looks like this:

222 122 221 — 16
212 212 223 — 17

This astounding 39-under-par figure consists of four double-eagles, 18 eagles and one birdie. In Eric Whitehead's excellent book on Capilano, "Hathstauwk", it is noted that McKinnon started this streak during the first round he ever played on the course, just a few weeks after his arrival from Scotland in 1937.

The finishing holes at Capilano have represented the turning point in many tournaments.

Architect Robert Trent Jones, Jr., was astounded at the magnificent mountain setting he was given at Chateau Whistler, as exemplified by the green setting at the 399-yard third hole.

CHATEAU WHISTLER

Golf Club

Public

Right from the moment you are greeted by attendants in caps and plus fours, you know you are in for a special treat at the Chateau Whistler Golf Club, designed by Robert Trent Jones, Jr. With an elevation change of 300 feet, this is true alpine golf, stretched around the base of Blackcomb Mountain in the heart of what must be considered Canada's finest collection of upscale public-access golf courses.

Joined by Big Sky Golf and Country Club, Whistler Golf Club, and Nicklaus North, Chateau Whistler rounds out a near-perfect golfing foursome at the quaint village, formerly renowned only for skiing, a couple of hours north of Vancouver. The golf course is also an ideal addition to the amenities offered by the Chateau Whistler hotel, one of the finest CP Hotels. In fact, the resort was voted by readers of *Conde Nast Traveler* as one of the best properties in the world and received a gold medal from *Golf Magazine*. The golf course itself was named the best new course in Canada by *Golf Digest* in 1993.

Although some may question the power of this spectacular layout with its relatively innocuous 6,600-yard length, they would be well served to notice the Slope rating of 142 from the men's championship tees. The Chateau Whistler course is a stern test of any player's shot-

Chateau Whistler: The par-3 eighth hole at Chateau Whistler is 212 yards from the gold tees, 184 from the blues, 158 from the whites, and 123 from the reds, making it accessible for players of all abilities. While it is a challenging shot, players are often distracted by the beauty surrounding them. The green sits some 80 feet below the tee and from that vantage point, you are tantalized with vistas of glaciers. Of course, don't forget about the water all the way down the left and the granite cliff on the right.

Chateau Whistler Golf Club
Whistler, British Columbia

	Length	Par
Gold	6635	72
Blue	6243	72
White	5692	72

Hole	Yards	Par			
1	505	5	10	131	3
2	326	4	11	355	4
3	399	4	12	395	4
4	411	4	13	349	4
5	190	3	14	352	4
6	457	4	15	389	4
7	538	5	16	167	3
8	212	3	17	444	4
9	472	5	18	543	5
OUT	3510	37	IN	3125	35
			Total	7140	72

The ruggedness of mountain courses lends itself to creating spectacular par 3s. Few are more breathtaking than the 190-yard fifth hole at Chateau Whistler.

making ability, winding through Douglas Firs, rocky outcrops, glacier-fed streams, and wildlife — including bears. No matter how many times you play here, you will face a challenge to concentrating on golf, so stunning is the scenery provided by the Coast Mountains. Should you lose your focus for a moment, never fear: Each cart is provided with a portable global positioning system which provides pinpoint yardages from your cart to the middle of the green, over creeks and bunkers, and so on. It also passes along other pertinent course information, such as the best angle from which to approach the green, the contours and speed of the putting surface, and hazards to avoid.

The architect took care to trace the natural pitches and valleys when routing this beauty; as a result, nine holes are played out from the clubhouse before the back nine brings you home. The 505-yard, par-5 opening hole is

Gaping bunkers, deep rough, and the unrelenting beauty of the surrounding mountains taxes even the best golfer's concentration on the 352-yard 14th hole at Chateau Whistler.

straightforward, allowing you to work the kinks out before negotiating the deceiving 326-yard second hole. Here you must steer the approach shot over a rugged creek to a well-protected green that slopes severely back toward the creek that guards it. Having survived that nerve-wracking experience, you are on the tee of the third hole, considered by many the best at Chateau Whistler. The 399 yards of this tree-lined dogleg left are magnified because they are all uphill. Brawn and brains are tested here, since the tee shot must be perfect to allow a clear shot at the green nestled in

a natural draw just over a portion of the Horstman River. The front of this green is the highest point of the course; at 2,530 feet above sea level, it is 300 feet above the first tee.

The par-3 fifth hole plays 190 yards downhill, while the tee shot on the supremely difficult par-4 sixth — at 457 yards it has earned its rank as the No. 1 handicap hole — must carry water yet again. The 528-yard seventh offers you a chance to catch your breath, or perhaps to have it snatched away once again in awe at the vista that is presented on the tee. That arousal of your senses will only be heightened, if that is possible, when you arrive at the next hole. Any course architect will attest that such savage topography lends itself to dramatic sites for breathtaking par 3s. Nowhere is this more apparent than at the 212-yard eighth hole which plays 80 feet downhill to a green bracketed by a crystal lake and a two-story granite rock face.

Another magnificent par 3 awaits after the short par-5 ninth hole, a dogleg right lined with majestic Douglas Firs and a string of fairway bunkers. Like the eighth, the much shorter 10th plays downhill amid granite rock faces and provides a stunning view of Green Lake hundreds of feet below. Then the course again heads uphill, with a run of five par 4s ranging in length from 395 to 349 yards. Although none of them inspires

fear with mere length, each presents a unique strategic challenge. For example, the 352-yard 14th is a classic risk-reward situation where the golfer must gamble on how much of the hazard he can carry on his way to the landing area.

The penultimate hole is a 444-yarder fraught with danger: enormous trees, bunkers, and water bisecting the fairway in front of the green. The relatively gentle par-5 18th allows your heart rate to return to normal after an exhilarating round.

A round at Chateau Whistler Golf Club is not inexpensive, but is certainly worth every penny. As architect Robert Trent Jones, Jr., says: "It was a tremendous design challenge, but the result speaks for itself."

Primeval forest and its denizens, including bears, are a constant at Chateau Whistler. Here, the par-4 13th hole.

*Architect Doug Carrick says he was so struck by
the natural green site that eventually became the
par-3 sixth hole that he designed the Greywolf
course around it.*

Panorama, British Columbia

GREYWOLF

Golf Course

Resort

"Greywolf is without question the most spectacular site I've ever worked with," says course architect Doug Carrick of Toronto. "There are unbelievable mountain views on every hole and almost 500 feet of elevation change on the golf course, including one hole that drops almost 200 feet from tee to green, and a par 3 across a 100-foot-deep canyon to a cliffside green at the base of a massive mountain peak."

Owned by Intrawest Corporation of Vancouver, British Columbia, which also owns other spectacular properties such as Whistler/Blackcomb in B.C. and Mont Tremblant in Quebec, Greywolf opened for limited play late in 1998.

"There are 18 signature holes at this course," says Carrick of the property, which winds through and around mountains, providing — appropriately enough — a panoramic view of various peaks and valleys. The course is bentgrass from tee to green and has water on 14 holes. Surprisingly, for a mountain course, a relatively small amount of rock was blasted, and the lion's share of that was at one hole.

Right from the first time he visited the site in January 1996 — "It was 30 below on the back of a snowmobile," he recalls with a grimace — Carrick knew this project was special. And the centrepiece had to be what eventually would become the 180-yard, par-3 sixth hole, now called

In the first three holes, Greywolf climbs about 250 feet
in elevation. This is the par-4 second hole.

Greywolf Golf Course
Panorama, British Columbia

	Length	Par
Black	7140	72
Gold	6627	72
White	6141	72

Hole	Yards	Par				
1	410	4		10	587	5
2	393	4		11	343	4
3	523	5		12	187	3
4	477	4		13	442	4
5	563	5		14	530	5
6	180	3		15	158	3
7	430	4		16	390	4
8	451	4		17	453	4
9	185	3		18	438	4
OUT	3612	36		IN	3528	36
				Total	7140	72

"Cliffhanger." Set across an alpine valley from the tee, the green site had to be knocked down about two metres in order to be more receptive, necessitating the removal of substantial bedrock.

"That green site stuck out the first time I saw the property. The most dramatic way to utilize it was to hit the tee shot across the canyon and have the green perched on the edge of the cliff. You've got a fabulous mountain backdrop behind the green and then if you look to the left of the green, you're looking up an unbelievably beautiful river valley that you can't see from the tee."

The remainder of the rock was blown out of the site of the 13th fairway, resulting in a rolling, rugged hole not unlike some at the brawny Highlands Links on Cape Breton Island, designed by the late Stanley Thompson. Interestingly, Carrick is in some ways the inheritor of Thompson's legacy, having partnered for a time with Robbie Robinson, Thompson's associate.

Although Carrick had previously worked with a wilderness setting at the spectacular Twin Rivers Golf Course in Newfoundland, he found new challenges at Panorama. "You really have a lot to work with, but the routing is tremendously important. That's everything. You have to work with the terrain, you can't fight it." As a result, the course rises about 250 feet in just the first three holes. Don't even think about walking at Greywolf.

Carrick struggles when asked to identify some special holes among these 18 beauties. No doubt the third hole is a contender. The drive on this uphill, 523-yard par 5 must clear a mountain stream that runs down the left side of the fairway before cutting in front of the tees. The second shot must either carry cross-bunkers on the right side of the fairway that angle toward the green, allowing an easy pitch to the elevated green, or face a

Greywolf: Even if you have played a lot of golf — even a lot of mountain golf — it is doubtful you have played a course with an elevation change of about 500 feet. As you stand on the fourth tee, you are at the highest point of the spectacular Greywolf Golf Course in British Columbia. Pull out the driver and let 'er rip, since the 150-foot drop to the landing area plus the thin air all but guarantees a career drive here. The fairway is receptive to all but the most errant shots and the green is easy to hit with a short iron.

The 587-yard, par-5 10th hole at Greywolf is appropriately named "Tranquillity."

The opening hole at spectacular Greywolf in the Canadian Rockies wends its way through an alpine valley.

tough shot over deep bunkers for those electing to stay left.

One of the benefits of mountain golf — aside from the scenery — is evident at the 477-yard, par-4 fourth hole. A 150-foot drop, abetted by the fact that the golf ball flies farther at this elevation, means this apparent monster is a driver-wedge for the better player. "This is a fun hole," says Carrick, "because the fairway is shaped like a big catcher's mitt, sort of bowled, so you can really let go on the tee."

Carrick repeatedly uses the word "fun" to describe Greywolf, with its generous fairways and receptive greens. Visually intimidating, it is very playable. "On every par 4 and every par 5, you can hit your driver without any real worries. The golf course looks much tougher than it plays." Kudos to Carrick and Intrawest for designing a layout appropriate for the clientele, who will mostly be tourists staying at the Panorama Village.

But that doesn't mean Greywolf, at 7,140 yards from the tips, won't eat up an unwary visitor, or any player who overestimates his or her ability. The fifth hole is a prime example. This reachable par 5 drops about 120 feet off the tee, with a sizable mountain stream that cuts across the fairway between the first and second landing areas on a right-to-left diagonal. "You can try to go straight at the green, carrying the creek," says Carrick, "or you can bail out to the right at many different angles, leaving yourself a tough downhill pitch to a little popup green with a bunker on the right. So, the further right you go, the worse angle you have into the green, so you really want to bite off as much of the river as you can. It's a great strategic par 5."

Panorama Village, the largest accommodation facility in the region, offers hotel and condominium accommodations, restaurants, shopping, an outdoor pool, river rafting, tennis, and a variety of other summer activities. The addition of this great golf course ensures the true four-season versatility of this mountain resort, already renowned for its alpine skiing. Interspersed throughout the course, but hopefully not intruding on it, will be homes reflecting the character of the old national park lodges and mountain chalets, with stone accents and rough-hewn timbers.

——— *Parksville, British Columbia* ———

MORNINGSTAR

International Golf Course

*Architect: Les Furber
General Manager: Deborah Zorkin
Head Professional: Joe Brien
Superintendent: Richard Donaldson*

The "International" in the official title of this spectacular course on Vancouver Island owes much, as does the very existence of the facility, to businessman Mladen Zorkin.

Zorkin, the farsighted mastermind behind this $20-million, 400-acre golf course/residential development which opened in 1991, was born in 1914 on the island of Dalmatia in the Balkans. He is reputed to speak 11 languages and served as a translator during the Second World War.

When the war ended, Zorkin was in London, England, when he stumbled across a book which contained "The Report of the British Admiralty of 1895." The report, says the urbane, debonair Zorkin, "mentioned the two best climates in the British Empire. One was in New Zealand and the other was the French Creek area around Parksville-Qualicum on Vancouver Island." The report mentioned no freezing for 365 days a year, 22 inches of rain and more than 2,000 hours of sunshine.

Although he arrived in Canada a couple of years later, it wasn't until 1961 that he made his way to his final destination. Now considered one of the most influential developers on the Island, his first venture 30 years ago was the 300-acre Columbia Estates development.

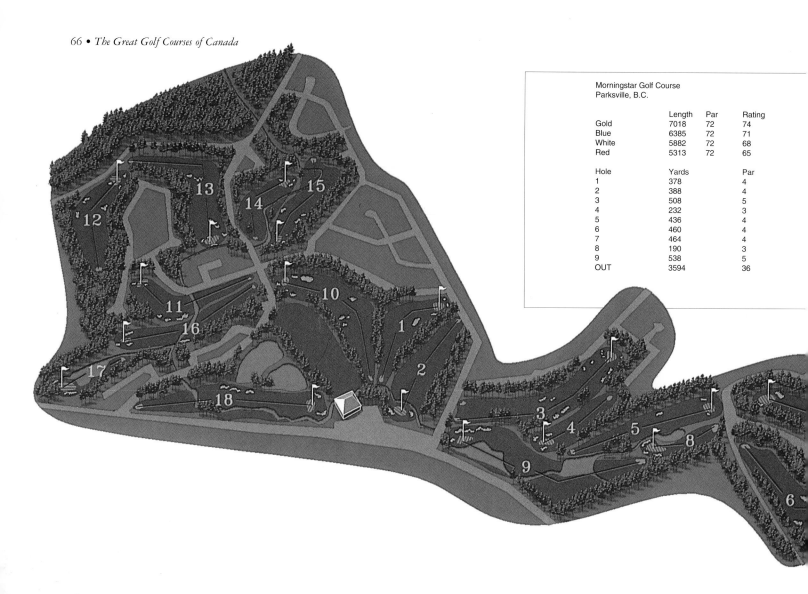

Morningstar Golf Course
Parksville, B.C.

	Length	Par	Rating
Gold	7018	72	74
Blue	6385	72	71
White	5882	72	68
Red	5313	72	65

Hole	Yards		Par
1	378		4
2	388		4
3	508		5
4	232		3
5	436		4
6	460		4
7	464		4
8	190		3
9	538		5
OUT	3594		36

A workaholic, Zorkin doesn't even play golf, but he was shrewd enough to realize how addictive the game can be. "Once you get into golf, you can't get out," he observes. Zorkin himself was hooked on the concept of a world-class golf course when he conceived the project in the 1960s. "People said we were crazy; we could have quit many times," he recalls. But his formula for success, proven many times over, is deceptively simple: "You always have to have the best location and the best facility and you can't fail. What you need is knowledge, ability, perseverance – and a good idea."

Obviously, Morningstar International Golf Course was a good idea: he has been offered $25 million for the facility by a group of offshore investors who wanted to make it an exclusive private enclave. "I would never sell the course because it would defeat the purpose," Zorkin says. "This is a golf course for everybody, not just for Vancouver Island, but for all of North America. My goal is to make Morningstar the best golf course in North America."

True to his word, it cost just $31 to play this public masterpiece in 1992. And the players who came here from around the globe to compete for a spot on the Canadian Professional Golf Tour at the 1992 qualifying school were unanimous in their assessment of Morningstar as "world class."

Zorkin's daughter, Deborah, is Morningstar's general manager and the golfer in the family. "We want to make it one of the top courses in North America, but we want to make it available to everybody. We can play it very hard (the course exceeds 7,000 yards from the back tees), or we can play it very reasonable, having our four and five tee block system. We want to show that we can have a first-class golf course that doesn't get burdened down with a membership. That's a real asset to tourism in the area."

Just as Zorkin makes an indelible impression on anyone he meets, he wants to ensure that every aspect of his course burns itself into a visitor's memory. The word

10	519	5
11	371	4
12	404	4
13	507	5
14	215	3
15	329	4
16	398	4
17	207	3
18	474	4
IN	3424	36
Total	7018	72

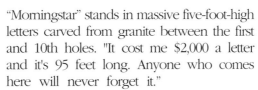

"Morningstar" stands in massive five-foot-high letters carved from granite between the first and 10th holes. "It cost me $2,000 a letter and it's 95 feet long. Anyone who comes here will never forget it."

Head pro Joe O'Brien agrees that a visit to Morningstar is unforgettable for a number of reasons. From a golfer's standpoint, O'Brien makes the following observations:

"Morningstar possesses a blend of links-style holes, open fairways and greenside bunkers. The fairways on many holes are completely isolated by trees, requiring straight, strategically placed shots in order to have a clear approach to the greens. It is rare that a day should pass without seeing a deer run across a fairway or one of the resident eagles soaring overhead."

O'Brien also offers some tips to the first-timer at Morningstar in a handy course guide available in the well-stocked pro shop. The first and most important is to manage your game well, playing intelligent shots to the appropriate spots on the fairway. The unforgiving towering trees which line almost every fairway will penalize the foolhardy.

The holes near the clubhouse are rela-

Number 17 offers water down the right side and a very tricky green.

The narrow fifth fairway at Morningstar demands accuracy.

tively open but almost every other hole on the course is cut out of the dense forest. The entire region is presided over by the Coastal Mountains, providing every shot at Morningstar with a breathtaking backdrop.

The area around Morningstar is fast becoming Canada's retirement capital. With year-round golf available to all residents, Morningstar offers a lifestyle previously thought to be found only in more southern climates. The housing development, covering 200 acres, will offer only 500 single-family homes in a forest setting only a five-minute walk from the Pacific Ocean. Once again, it appears the remarkable Dr. Zorkin has a jump on the competition!

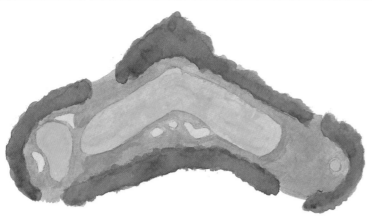

The Toughest Hole at Morningstar

The seventh hole at Morningstar is rated the toughest on the course. It's a long dogleg-left which plays to 464 yards from the gold tees, 434 from the blues, 406 from the whites and 374 from the red blocks. The ideal tee shot is long and straight down the right side of the fairway to avoid the cluster of fairway bunkers on the left, in the corner of the dogleg. A fairway wood or long iron must be struck perfectly to get to the 6,000-square-foot green which is guarded by bunkers. A par 4 here is remarkable.

Number 9, a double-dogleg par 5, has it all: length, lakes, hollows and bunkers.

*A stunning 185-yard par 3 kicks off
the back nine at Nicklaus North.*

NICKLAUS NORTH

Golf Course

Semi-Private

Jack Nicklaus has had mixed luck in Canada. A seven-time
runner-up record in the Canadian Open, including a couple of
bridesmaid finishes on a golf course he designed — Glen
Abbey in Oakville, Ontario — might have left a bit of a sour
taste for the Great White North.

But he managed to overlook that blip in his otherwise historic career when he was approached to design an upscale golf
course in the spectacular Rocky Mountain resort village of
Whistler, British Columbia, about two hours north of
Vancouver. And while it doesn't make up for missing out on
the national Open championship, the list of accolades garnered
by Nicklaus North since it opened in August 1995 must be
extremely gratifying for the Golden Bear. *Golf Digest* named it
the best new golf course in Canada in 1996 and the British
Columbia Professional Golfers' Association designated it as
the Golf Facility of the Year in 1997.

Built on 145 acres of valley flatlands bordered by glacier-fed Green Lake, Nicklaus North was only the second golf course in the world that the greatest golfer of all time deigned to lend his surname to. It was an appropriate choice, since the 6,900-yard layout has proved to be an enjoyable test for not only tourists, but also for Fred Couples, Greg Norman, Nick Faldo, and Nicklaus himself when the 1997 Export 'A' Skins Game was played here. For the record, Norman won 13 skins worth $275,000, Couples was second with three skins and $50,000, followed by Nicklaus with two skins and $35,000. Faldo was shut out.

Cognizant of the clientele attracted to the Whistler area to play some of the country's finest courses — Whistler Golf Club, Chateau Whistler Golf Club, Big Sky Golf and Country Club and Nicklaus North — the layout is scenically over-whelming but extremely playable. Five sets of tees range from 6,900 to 4,700 yards, making this course a pleasure to play for any handicap level. Nicklaus used phrases such as "fun golf," "not very severe," and "plenty of area to play" when describing his award-winning design. Plenty of area, indeed: Some fairways are more than 100 yards wide and the enormous greens have none of the roller-coaster contours that characterized some of Nicklaus's earlier works. Almost 60 white-sand scalloped bunkers protect these putting surfaces and there is water on 15 holes.

While the entire Nicklaus North experience is an uplifting one, much ado has been made about its finishing holes, commencing with the 15th, a 437-yard par 4 abutting Green Lake on the left. (Green Lake actually has a greenish hue, due to mineral deposits caused by the

At 226 yards, the par-3 17th hole has a terrifying array of hazards in addition to sheer length: sand, water, and a tough green.

melting glacier that drains into the lake.) Bending slightly from right to left, the tee shot must carry a pond on its route to the undulating fairway. A brace of fairway bunkers awaits an errant tee shot. A huge bunker lurks to the right of the kidney-shaped green.

Fitzsimmons Creek bisects the fairway of the par-4 16th hole about 100 yards short of the green, which is guarded on the left by a capacious amoeba-shaped bunker and on the right by trees. Another distraction on this hole is the sight of floatplanes docking just a few yards from the clubhouse.

The 226-yard, par-3 17th hole, set at the base of snow-capped Wedge Mountain, is referred to as the signature hole at Nicklaus North. The last of the

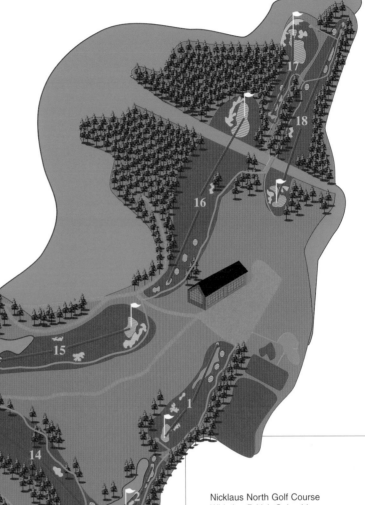

Nicklaus North Golf Course
Whistler, British Columbia

	Length	Par
Gold	6908	71
Blue	6413	71
White	6004	71

Hole	Yards	Par
1	390	4
2	197	3
3	518	5
4	465	4
5	416	4
6	179	3
7	366	4
8	514	5
9	376	4
OUT	3421	36
10	185	3
11	555	5
12	225	3
13	564	5
14	432	4
15	437	4
16	425	4
17	226	3
18	438	4
IN	3487	35
Total	6908	71

Nicklaus North: (7th hole) This straightforward, 366-yard par 4 plays directly into the wind. From the tee, the player is faced with some ominous bunkering. A well-placed tee shot will leave a short iron to the deep, narrow green. This beautifully designed hole captures the scenic magnificence of Whistler Mountain.

The 16th fairway is bisected by water, threatening the approach shot on the 425-yard par 4.

five one-shotters here, it requires a long carry over Green Lake to a green hugged on three sides by a bunker which could stop over-exuberant tee shots from meeting a watery fate. The hole itself was created by dumping thousands of tons of boulders into the lake.

The 18th, a sturdy par 4, also features Fitzsimmons Creek cutting in front of the green. A lone fairway bunker provides a visual aiming device for the tee shot, which should touch down on the right side of the fairway to provide the optimal angle of attack on the green.

Recognizing environmental sensitivity as a priority after substantial local opposition to the project, Nicklaus North undertook a number of environmental studies during the course of its development. The Golden Bear Group, Nicklaus's design company, along with the landscape architect, environmental consultants, and the project manager, hosted a series of workshops to address environmental concerns from which evolved a vegetation and habitat management plan. The plan integrated the golf course design into the existing terrain using a topographical map taken from aerial photos. The map, along with prototypical planting plans, environmental auditing plans, special habitat-enhancement programs and plant species, was integrated into a reference manual that will be used as a guideline for similar undertakings.

So, in addition to adding a great course to Canada's inventory of golf facilities, Nicklaus North contributed a great deal to the understanding of how golf can co-exist with the natural environment.

The front nine at Nicklaus North concludes with a 376-yard par 4 which skirts the glacier-fed Green Lake.

PREDATOR RIDGE

Golf Resort

Architect: Les Furber
Head Professional: Sandy Kurceba
General Manager: Barrie Wheeler
Superintendent: Jim Barker

Predator Ridge Golf Resort is about a 15-minute drive south of Vernon in British Columbia's picturesque Okanagan Valley. The exact location is called "the commonage," the common area used by the local ranchers to herd cattle from Lake Kalamalka to Lake Okanagan.

The region's high, rolling hills and serpentine valleys provide the perfect landscape for a golf course. It was in 1988 when Herb and Dave Patterson of Toronto first viewed the site. The Patterson family, prominent members of the Canadian golf industry since the 1950's as the distributor for Titleist golf equipment, were aware of the rapid growth in golf and saw an opportunity to establish a world-class golf facility in the B.C. Interior.

"We knew there was growth in the area because a great barometer for golf is the sale of golf balls," says co-owner Barrie Wheeler, who formerly worked with the Patersons. "Herb had built St. Andrews East (described in the Ontario section of this book) and St. Andrews Valley and I told him, 'Don't forget your old friend when you build a third.'

"I was very impressed when I saw the area and I knew Herb would do a great job. So we bought it in 1989, and we knew it was an exceptional piece of property, ideally suited for a golf course."

Predator Ridge got its name from the lynx, bobcats and coyotes that roam its forests, but an unwary golfer can get eaten alive by the layout which calls for precise shotmaking. Architect Les Furber of Canmore, Alberta, worked on the design which will eventually comprise 36 holes.

"We knew that Les Furber had been with Robert Trent Jones for 14 years and was one of Jone's key men," recalls Wheeler. "So we knew quite a bit about Les Furber's work and that he built courses in a very similar style to those of Trent Jones. We're very pleased with the job he did here."

Furber, who has developed into one of Canada's best known course architects, utilized the natural roll of the terrain, the rocks, bluffs and lakes in designing the course, the end result being a facility that fits well with the local environment and enhances the surrounding landscape. The design philosophy developed with the owners was to intigrate the course into the convoluted terrain. "We walked the terrain with Les a lot," says Wheeler, "and agreed to work with the terrain rather than fight it."

One of the more unique features of Predator Ridge that Furber built into the design are the bentgrass target landing areas in the fairways. Wheeler thinks this course is the first in Canada to use the technique.

"Of course, now that I've said it's the first, I'll probably get calls from another course that has it, but it's very rare. It defines the landing area and gives you a beautiful target to aim at."

In addition to the brilliant green target areas, the course boasts silica bunker sand and "probably one of the largest irrigation systems ever installed," Wheeler adds. "We have 1,250 sprinklers and nearly 250 kilometres of underground piping and wire which is absolutely essential here."

The existing 18 holes are a composite of holes from the eventual 36-hole layout. Eventually, one course will remain public while the other will be exclusively for member play. "We had 30,000 rounds this year and when we hit 40,000 rounds we may complete another nine," says Wheeler, "and then we will add another nine to take it up to 36."

Plans include an expanded clubhouse for 1993 and possibly a residential development, Wheeler adds. "We've tried to have something different here at Predator Ridge, with

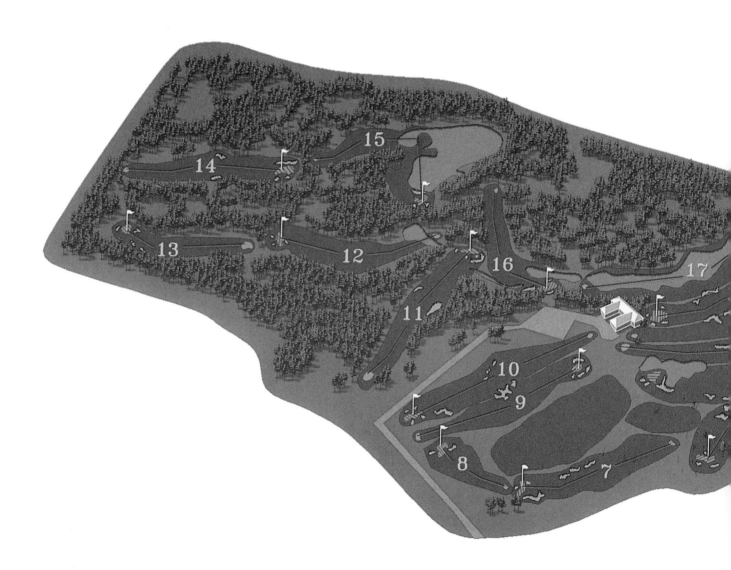

At 460 yards, the 15th is the longest par 4 at Predator Ridge.

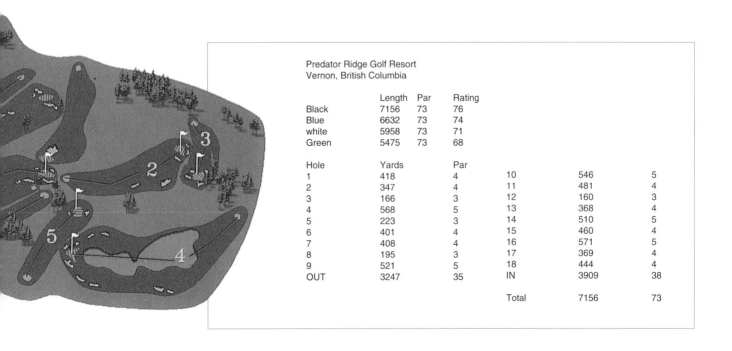

Predator Ridge Golf Resort
Vernon, British Columbia

	Length	Par	Rating
Black	7156	73	76
Blue	6632	73	74
white	5958	73	71
Green	5475	73	68

Hole	Yards	Par			
1	418	4	10	546	5
2	347	4	11	481	4
3	166	3	12	160	3
4	568	5	13	368	4
5	223	3	14	510	5
6	401	4	15	460	4
7	408	4	16	571	5
8	195	3	17	369	4
9	521	5	18	444	4
OUT	3247	35	IN	3909	38
			Total	7156	73

The tee shot on 12 must carry a lake to reach the well-protected green.

valet parking, lessons and good people on staff. People seem to enjoy coming here to golf."

Head pro Sandy Kurceba is reticent to identify the toughest hole on the course, maintaining that each has its own character and challenge. "Number 7 is the toughest according to the scorecard, but Number 4 is probably the toughest to play."

The feared fourth is a par 5 with everything, the pro boasts. It's got sand, water, out of bounds and a large kidney-shaped green. It also has a double carry over water. The situation of the tee forces the average golfer to drive over a large pond. Those who lack nerve can aim for one of the closer landing areas and then work their way to the green.

The seventh also features a dogleg. The second shot will make or break your score on this hole. Take an extra club because you must fly the ball all the way over a gully at the front of the shallow green. "You have to get the ball airborne," says Kurceba, "you can't run it in."

Kurceba itemizes each hole, pointing out the intricacies of Furber's design. "Number 13, nicknamed Duffer's Delight, is probably the easiest to score on. It allows for a downhill tee shot to a wide-open, flat landing area." But, as with every hole at Predator Ridge, there is a catch. "The second shot is across a water hazard to a five-tiered green which is well protected by water."

Predator Ridge tested the mettle of the Canadian Tour's best players in the 1993 Xerox B.C. Open, a tribute to the calibre of such a new course.

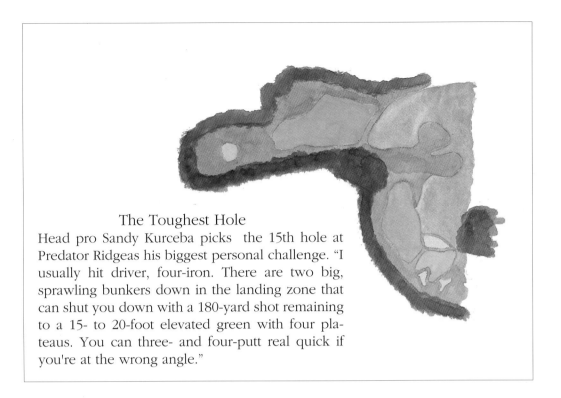

The Toughest Hole

Head pro Sandy Kurceba picks the 15th hole at Predator Ridgeas his biggest personal challenge. "I usually hit driver, four-iron. There are two big, sprawling bunkers down in the landing zone that can shut you down with a 180-yard shot remaining to a 15- to 20-foot elevated green with four pla-teaus. You can three- and four-putt real quick if you're at the wrong angle."

At 223 yards from the back tee, the 5th hole at Predator Ridge is a strong par 3.

—— *Victoria, British Columbia* ——

VICTORIA

Golf Club

Architect: A. V. Macan
Head Professional: Mike Parker
Manager: Don Francis
Superintendent: Alec Kazai

If you've heard rumors of a fantastic, mysterious golf links on Vancouver Island called Oak Bay, this is it. It has been officially known as the Victoria Golf Club since 1893, the year a band of hardy hackers rented farmland surrounded on two sides by the ocean and proceeded to lay out 11 holes. The club is the oldest in the Pacific Northwest still in existence, followed by the Tacoma Club (1894) in the neighboring state of Washington.

In his book, A Guide to the Golf Courses of British Columbia, Alan Dawe says, "Tradition has it that members of the Victoria Golf Club eventually had to buy this property because the farmers they leased it from had the unfortunate habit of driving all golfers off the fairways during the summer months so that their cows and sheep could safely graze."

If true, then that was the last time that anyone or anything forced the membership off

its links. Fiercely proud of its reputation as "the" golf club on Vancouver Island, this very private establishment is equally proud of its course — and justifiably so.

However, says Head Professional Mike Parker, if anything could push a golfer off this layout, it would be the wind. "You're right on the ocean and the wind is very much a factor," says Parker. The back tee for the par-three ninth hole is on a postage-stamp of land leaning into the ocean and new members are baptized by the spray crashing over the tee. "Sometimes you have to have someone hold your ball on the tee," says the pro, "otherwise it will blow off. Timing is very important on this shot!" On the preceding hole, a 115-yarder, Parker has hit a wedge on still days — and a hard three-iron when faced with a winter gale. Facing a winter gale is not unusual at the Victoria Golf Club. Parker says the course is open more days than any other in Canada, due to the moderate climate of southern Vancouver Island which allows golfing year-round.

Those foolish enough to write off this course as a pushover because the card reveals a length from the back tees of just over 6,000 yards are in for a rude awakening. Since positioning is vital on this narrow, devious design routed through just 97 rolling acres, it may be wise to give the driver a day off. Irons from the tee are the rule here with only a few exceptions, a situation that makes the golf course seem longer. In addition, a modern irrigation system tends to prevent any significant roll. "In large part," says Parker, "the irrigation has taken away a lot of the bump-and-run aspect of this course. Now players can fly the ball into the greens and they will hold the shot. I know players who say they used to drive the 18th

At only 145 yards, the second hole rates the nickname "Calamity."

Victoria Golf Club
Victoria, British Columbia

	Length	Par	Rating
Blue	6015	70	69
White	5857	71	68

Hole	Yards	Par
1	502	5
2	145	3
3	402	4
4	362	4
5	324	4
6	341	4
7	369	4
8	115	3
9	194	3
OUT	2754	34
10	350	4
11	438	5
12	521	5
13	158	3
14	194	3
15	404	4
16	356	4
17	450	5
18	390	4
IN	3261	37
Total	6015	71

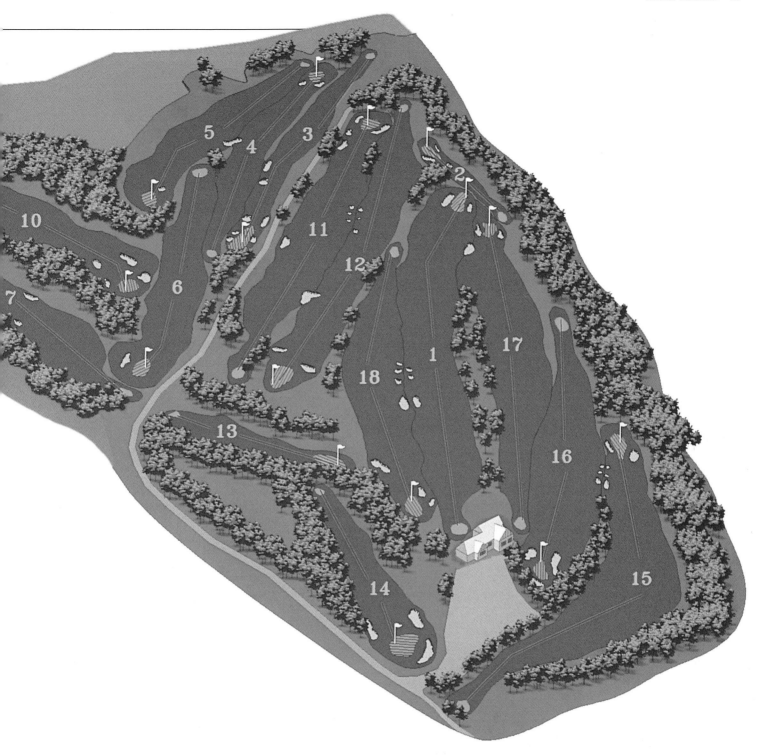

green (390 yards) in the days before irrigation, when the fairways were hard and fast. Now if you're within a hundred yards of the green, you're a hero."

Parker says the first two holes at Victoria Golf Club are reasonable warm-ups, even though the first hole is a 500-yard par-five into that notorious wind. The third hole is rated the toughest on the course and a hint of what's to come is found in its name: the Road Hole. Like its excruciatingly difficult namesake at the Old Course at St. Andrews in Scotland, a roadway figures in the layout.

But in this case, the road is Beach Drive, which trails along the left boundary of the hole. The fairway is not wide, but downwind, fortunately. Use a driver or three-wood off the tee and you will be left with a mid-iron into a three-level green that is 40 yards deep. Obviously, there is some anxiety involved in club selection for that second shot.

Once on the green, there is still much work to be done, for Victoria is touted to have the fastest greens in the West. In general, they are not large, although they do vary in size. They are characterized by undulations that are

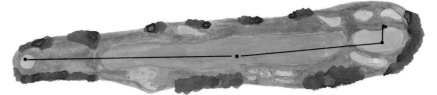

Hole #11: 438 yards par 4

The Toughest Hole at Victoria

Though it's rated the Number 2 stroke hole, Head Professional Mike Parker calls the 11th hole at the Victoria Golf Club the most difficult on the course. It's a 438-yard par-four from the blue tees (a 458-yard par-five from the whites) and epitomizes the course's emphasis on positioning and pinpoint accuracy. "You have to play this into the wind and there's out-of-bounds all down the left side. Take a long-iron off the tee and you've still got a very difficult second shot. If you hit two good ones, you deserve to make par, and the green reflects that because it's one of the most level surfaces on the golf course."

Victoria's seaside setting contributes to its "links" atmosphere.

No. 5 is a short but exquisitely beautiful par-four.

reminiscent of the waves crashing into the nearby shore. Instead of swales, tiers and humps, one thinks of the greens as possessing breakers, combers, rollers and chutes; the putting surfaces are that idiosyncratic. "There are very few flat lies," confirms Parker. "We find it compensates for the length." Without a doubt.

The fifth hole, appropriately called The Bay, is a shortish par-four notable for two things: a very quick green even by Victoria Golf Club standards, and the start of a spectacular stretch of holes parallel to the ocean. The next hole, Vimy Ridge, forces the player to hit a blind tee shot over the ridge onto a plateau. From there, he must hit another blind shot to a green some 10 metres below the level of the fairway. "A members' hole," concedes Parker.

If you don't feel up to playing the seventh hole as a par-four, you have the option of playing it as the par-three it used to be, thanks to some novel course renovations several years ago. The ocean comes into play on the left from the tee all the way to a very severe green.

The back nine provides no respite. Hit a one- or two-iron off the tee of the 350-yard 10th hole and, if you can battle the left-to-right sloping fairway and the wind which pushes the ball right, then you will have anything from a six-iron to a wedge in. Number 12 is the first of two par-fives on the back nine. The three-level green is severely trapped with pot bunkers and mounding, making it advisable to lay up on the second shot and try to knock your third tight to the pin position of the day.

The 13th and 14th holes are par-threes, but the latter is superior, especially from the back tee which is elevated. You have no option but to hit to the green that slopes away from you — there is no fairway, and out-of-bounds lurks left, right and over the green. Your trials continue until the 17th, which Parker admits is a "members' par-five." A birdie opportunity is treasured at Victoria.

At Westwood Plateau's short, par-4 second hole, a driver is not the best choice off the tee. Play for position instead, to ensure a precise shot into the small green

Coquitlam, British Columbia

WESTWOOD PLATEAU

Golf and Country Club

Public

"From your first welcome at our bag drop to your last putt on the 18th green, we are dedicated to making your time spent here memorable," says Jim McLaughlin, general manager of golf operations at Westwood Plateau. And one visit is all it takes to realize that McLaughlin and his staff pay much more than lip service to those words.

In fact, McLaughlin's unique approach to customer service has made Westwood Plateau in suburban Vancouver the envy of the Canadian golf industry. He and his staff seem positively infected with the urgent need to ensure every guest has the golfing experience of a lifetime.

Of course, it helps that Westwood Plateau is no mere golf course. Opened in 1995, it was selected the best new course in the country by *SCORE* magazine, while *Golf Digest* awarded it a four-star Good Service Award rating in its *Places To Play* publication. Those honours came as no surprise to anyone who is

Another of Westwood Plateau's tough par 3s. The 196-yard sixth hole calls for careful club selection. Aim at the righthand bunker to avoid the pit that guards the entire left side of the green.

familiar with the work of the course's architect, the renowned Michael Hurdzan of Columbus, Ohio, who also designed Le Diable in Quebec and the Devil's Pulpit and Paintbrush courses in Ontario.

"Westwood Plateau is another reminder of the incredible versatility of [Hurdzan]," says no less an authority than Ron Whitten, *Golf Digest*'s architectural editor. "I think he has taken his place among the best designers in the world."

Hurdzan incorporated massive Douglas Firs, imposing granite rock faces, rugged ravines, and breathtaking green sites into 18 great golf holes, some of which make the word "spectacular" seem inadequate.

"The ideal esthetic is to touch every sense and at Westwood Plateau, I believe we have done that," Hurdzan says of his creation. "A good golf course should be a total sensory experience where the land communicates with the golfer. You want to give the golfer what I call the 'Wow!' effect on every shot."

It doesn't take long for the first-time visitor to say "Wow!" — or something stronger. The relatively short opening hole welcomes the unwary neophyte with a par or birdie before the second hole comes into view, with the majestic mountains dwarfing the green. Playing for position on this shortish par 4 will be rewarded with the opportunity to drop a short-iron shot close to the pin on the small, slightly elevated green. Walking to the third tee is where Hurdzan's "Wow!" factor really comes into play. At 205 yards from the championship "Crown" tees, this uphill par 3 is a physical and psychological challenge. The ideal tee shot must carry a cavernous ravine and the prudent player will go up at least one club, and possibly two.

The par-4 fifth hole plays a brawny 470 yards from the tips down to a green protected by a creek in front and a monstrous greenside bunker on the right. Club selection is again paramount, since the green is

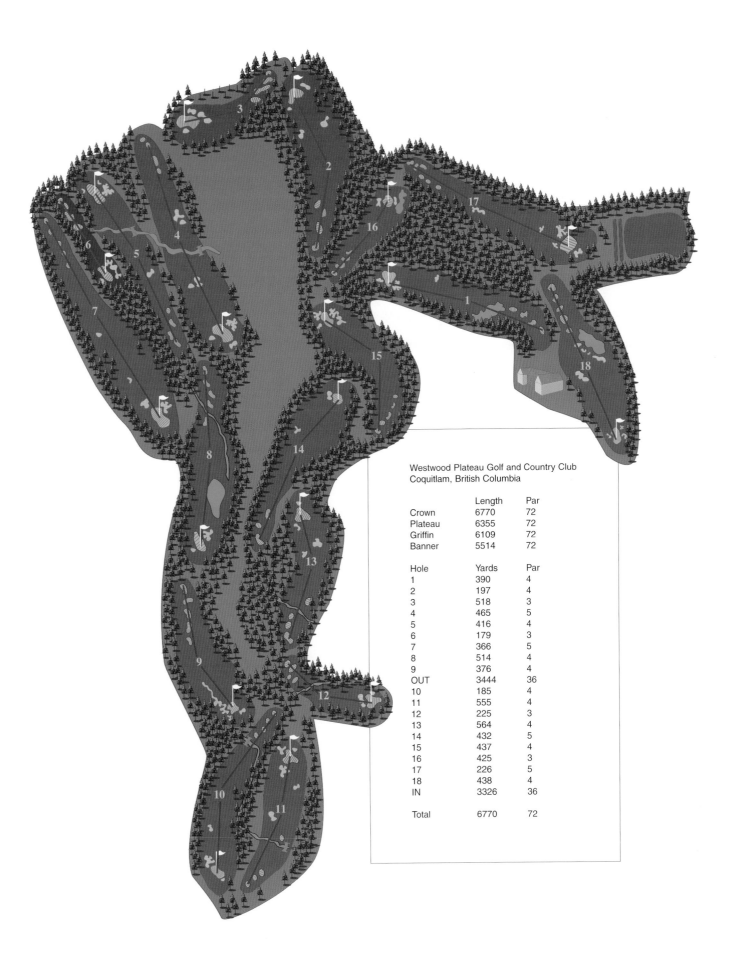

Westwood Plateau Golf and Country Club
Coquitlam, British Columbia

	Length	Par
Crown	6770	72
Plateau	6355	72
Griffin	6109	72
Banner	5514	72

Hole	Yards	Par
1	390	4
2	197	4
3	518	3
4	465	5
5	416	4
6	179	3
7	366	5
8	514	4
9	376	4
OUT	3444	36
10	185	4
11	555	4
12	225	3
13	564	4
14	432	5
15	437	4
16	425	3
17	226	5
18	438	4
IN	3326	36
Total	6770	72

The 382-yard 10th represents the toughest driving hole at Westwood Plateau. The green's setting has been termed "edge of the world" with good reason.

some 50 feet deep. After the pretty par-3 sixth hole, you come face to face with the No. 1 handicap hole at Westwood Plateau. Almost 600 yards from the back tees, it earns its title by forcing the player to hit three superb shots in order to get close to the hole in regulation. The ideal drive will head for the fairway bunker on the right side of the fairway. The front nine concludes with a short but devious par 4 that features almost as much sand as grass. Ripping a drive down the left side may be rewarded with a birdie, but even the slightest miscalculation will result in a bogey or worse.

The back nine opens with what the Westwood Plateau people call an "edge-of-the-world" green site, with the putting surface appearing to be precariously perched on a cliff and in danger of tumbling off. But you must keep focussed here, since the 10th is the most demanding driving hole on the course. No. 12 is another "wow" hole; the mid-length par 3 possesses a stunning green complex, backed up against a monumental granite rock face. Once again, it is

tough to concentrate, but you must — there is little room for error and a poor shot is punished severely.

Better players will be salivating when they walk onto the 14th tee, sensing that this downhill and shortish par 5 could provide them with an eagle opportunity. While that may be optimistic, a birdie is likely here, but not if you hit your approach shot over the green. The subsequent hole is a long par 4, but offers tremendous visual stimuli. There is a 150-foot drop from the back tee to the fairway which is bisected by a deep creek about 150 yards from the green. The 16th is the final par 3 at Westwood Plateau, playing from an elevated tee across a pond to a green guarded both left and right by sand.

After negotiating at least a par on the par-5 17th hole, which is only 501 yards from the tips, you can unleash the driver on the generous 18th fairway. Of course, since this fairway used to be the home stretch of the defunct Westwood Racetrack, you shouldn't be expected to "rein it in."

Westwood Plateau features much

Westwood Plateau: Architect Michael Hurdzan is justifiably proud of his creation at Westwood Plateau, and makes many mentions of it in his tremendous book, *Golf Course Architecture: Design, Construction and Restoration.* In particular, he singles out the site for what he calls "edge of the world" green settings. Some,

like the 10th, truly appear to hang over the lip of a cliff. Others, like the par-3 12th (pictured), abut massive stone out-croppings. To the architect's credit, he visualized the end result when confront-ed with solid granite. Extensive blasting was required to create the green site, but few trees were removed.

more than its superb 18-hole course. A par-31, nine-hole course with three tee decks, ranging from 1,805 to 1,330 yards, provides an opportunity for begin-ners to learn the game or more advanced players to hone their skills. The course roams over hilly terrain, presenting golfers with an exciting layout and won-derful views of the Fraser River Valley, and can be played in less than two hours.

The short, par-4 first hole at Westwood Plateau is a gentle wel-come to your round. Two decent shots should reward you with no less than a par, but take nothing for granted on any hole here.

*Club selection is paramount on
Algonquin's par-3 third hole.*

THE ALGONQUIN

Golf Course

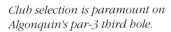

Architect: Donald Ross
Head Professional: Lindon Garron
General Manager: Jim Frise
Superintendent: Leon Harvey

So prominent is the reputation of the stately Algonquin Resort that many people do not realize that its terra-cotta turrets and gables are part of a spectacular horizon over the tree tops along many of the 27 fine golf holes.

Built in 1889, the hotel has expanded recently, adding a 15,000-square-foot convention centre and 50 new guest rooms and suites. The tradition-laden Algonquin — renowned for its hospitality, cuisine, accommodations and healthy climate — has been enjoyed by generations of guests who visit for fun-filled vacations or memorable conferences. The year it opened, the local newspaper proclaimed in words that ring as true today: "To the summer visitors, a hearty welcome! Let their stay be short or long, let them come in the fifties or the thousands, the welcome which awaits them will be nonetheless cordial."

The tradition of the golf course parallels — indeed precedes — that of the resort itself. In 1890, the hotel owners constructed six holes in front of the hotel. In 1894, the painter, Sir William Hope, and Mr. Allen, a civil engineer from Montreal, joined up with the St. Andrews Land Co. to build nine holes behind the hotel. History will congratulate them for their foresight in hiring

Optimistic players will try to drive the 16th, a short par 4.

The Algonquin Golf Course
St. Andrews By-The-Sea, New Brunswick

	Length	Par	Rating
Blue	6546	72	70
White	6226	72	69
Red (Ladies)	5503	74	73

Hole	Yards	Par				
1	429	4	10	317	4
2	478	5	11	524	5
3	157	3	12	373	4
4	373	4	13	556	5
5	414	4	14	419	4
6	308	4	15	193	3
7	135	3	16	312	4
8	328	4	17	376	4
9	400	4	18	422	4
OUT	3054	35	IN	3492	37
			Total	6546	72

the revered architect Donald Ross to lay out these holes which were situated where the present holes 4 through 12 are located.

In 1900, they purchased land to construct nine more holes, which lay where 2, 3, 14, 15, 16 and 17 are now. These were laid out from Donald Ross plans by John Peacock, who became the first club manager and head professional.

A few years later, Canadian Pacific (led by T.G. Shaughnessy, who was to lend his name to a notable golf course in Vancouver) purchased the holdings of the St. Andrews Land Co., specifically the hotel and golf course. In 1916, the owners decided to lengthen the course and purchased the Poor House Farm. It is on this land that today's first and 18th holes are located.

On what remained of the Poor House Farm property, a 2,025-yard, nine-hole course was built in 1921-22. It features narrow fairways and small greens.

While anyone, no matter what their recreational preference, is guaranteed the vacation of a lifetime in the Algonquin Resort, head pro Lindon Garron says the 18-hole Seaside Course will provide all golfers with shotmaking challenges. The course also de-livers breathtaking vistas since 13 holes are played on the banks of Passamaquoddy Bay, the arm of the sea which surrounds St. Andrews.

The first hole, a 429-yard par 4, plays long into prevailing winds. A row of trees on the right extends into the fairway about 250 yards out, making an approach tough from that side. Your second shot is blind. "Very seldom can anyone hit it far enough to see the flag," says Garron. The downhill second shot requires a wood to a flat green.

The 478-yard second hole "has been described as the most difficult hole," says Garron, "but if you guard against going out of bounds on the left, especially near the green where it narrows, it's a very easy par 5." The right side of the fairway slopes into the trees and trouble.

Hitting a long iron over water can cause the faint of heart some palpitations on the 189-yard, par-3 third. Take enough club to clear the hazard, but not too much, since more trouble lurks in the bunkers behind the green. The fourth hole is aptly numbered since its near-impossible green often leads to four putts. And the fifth hole holds a special place in Garron's heart (see sidebar).

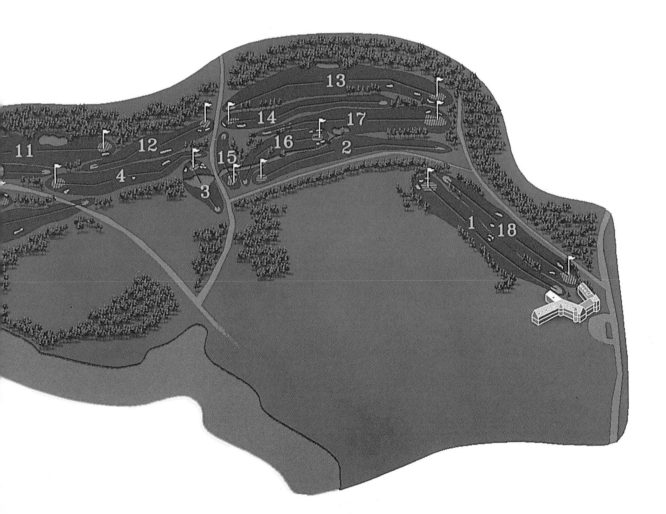

On Number 6, it is extremely easy to drive the ball into the ditch on the left. The second shot is to a tricky elevated green. On seven, says Garron, "the shot you make here is the reverse of the second shot you make on six. Here you are hitting downhill and the wind really affects the ball because you hit it so high."

The toughest part about the eighth hole is the second shot, the pro says. "It's usually a short shot, but the green slopes right to left and falls away from the golfer, so everything tends to run off the green." The front nine concludes with a 400-yard par 4 with a rise that starts at the landing area so even big hitters have a long approach shot.

The 10th is a short par 4 that compensates for its 317-yard length with a undulating, narrow, sloping green. The driver comes out of the bag on 11, a 524-yard par 5 that requires three shots for most players. On 12, Garron observes that "most drives will end up in the gully and leave you with

The Pro's Favorite

"Number 5 is one of my favorites," says Algonquin head professional Lindon Garron of this 414-yard par 4. "You get a fantastic view on both shots. When you hit off the tee, you, you're looking across the entrance of the St. Croix River and into Maine, and when you hit your second shot, you're looking out into Passamaquoddy Bay. It's much more difficult from the blue tees because you can barely get it to the corner of the sharp dogleg. The fairway starts to slope to the left at about the landing area. So, if you were to hit two similar drives, one hit down the left centre could be 40 to 50 yards farther than a ball hit to right centre. So it is possible to roll a ball around the corner."

an uphill blind second shot. The bunkers in front of the green are very deep."

On 13, the No. 1 rated hole at Algonquin, three shots are again required for all but the longest hitters. Out of bounds threatens all along the left side, and a clump of trees on the right must be avoided off the drive. Garron says 14 is one of the easiest holes on the course although plans call for the tee to be moved back to lengthen the hole to about 400 yards.

Fifteen is a good downhill par 3, where you can see the flagstick but not the green from the tee. Anything hit to the right side of the green will run into the pond. And on the 312-yard 16th, the long-hitting gambler will try to drive the green over the trees. It all depends where you stand against par at this point. Number 17 presents another blind shot where you can see the pin but not the surface of the long and narrow green. A shot

missed to the left or right drops off, making for a tough chip and putt for par.

"Number 18 is the most difficult hole on the golf course," says Garron. "The fairway is fairly wide, but you're driving uphill and there's out of bounds all the way down the left side. Your first 210 yards are uphill so if you don't hit a good drive, you're hitting into the hill. You immediately start to think about guarding your last drive of the day from going out of bounds, while knowing you have to hit it a long way to be able to get home in two shots. It's about the same length as Number 1, but the wind always seems to be against you."

With some skill and luck, you will card a 5 on Number 18 and then make your way back to the clubhouse or the hotel where a pint and a lobster dinner will put the finishing touches on another splendid day at one of Canada's finest golf resorts.

If you avoid the ditch on the left of Number 6, you still have to face a critical second shot.

Viewed from any perspective, the par-3 eighth hole at Bell Bay presents a challenge. The downhill 181-yarder allows no bailout, protected as it is by three good bunkers.

BELL BAY

Golf Club

Semi-Private

How good is Bell Bay? Good enough to be selected by *Golf Digest* as Canada's best new course in 1998. Good enough to be a fitting stablemate for Highlands Links, situated across Nova Scotia's Cape Breton Island and considered by many to be the best golf course in the country. And good enough, in the minds of some, to serve as the prototypical golf course for the 21st century because it is so user friendly.

The honour conferred upon Bell Bay by *Golf Digest* completed the hat trick for Thomas McBroom, Canada's marquee course architect. He also won in 1997 (Lake Joseph Club, Port Sandfield, Ont.) and 1994 (Links at Crowbush Cove, Morell,

P.E.I.). He was runner-up in 1996 (Le Géant, Mont Tremblant, Que.) and 1992 (Camelot Golf Club, Cumberland, Ont.).

More than adding another honour to McBroom's trophy case, Bell Bay illustrates the evolution of an architect's craft. Lost in his past and best forgotten are several early designs that give a very weak hint of the 46-year-old Toronto native's talents.

McBroom, who graduated with a degree in landscape architecture from the University of Guelph, obviously benefited from working with Robert Cupp of Georgia, who was deeply involved in the design of Glen Abbey Golf Club although Jack Nicklaus is generally given full credit.

The first hole at Bell Bay is a welcoming par 4 which doglegs gently to the right. The hole is named "Alexander" after the area's most famous resident, Alexander Graham Bell.

Cupp took McBroom under his wing on a couple of notable projects in Ontario: Beacon Hall in Aurora (1988) and Deerhurst Highlands in Huntsville (1990). In his time with Cupp, McBroom honed his skills, learning to emphasize the artistry, balance, and intuition that are an architect's stock in trade.

"With Bell Bay, McBroom goes from being a rising star in golf design to a headliner," said Ron Whitten, architecture editor for *Golf Digest*. "[Bell Bay] reemphasizes what an impressive repertoire he has tucked in his sketch pad."

Bell Bay is not as spectacular as Lake Joseph or Crowbush Cove, but it represents a purer distillation of the attributes that make a good course great. In many ways it is McBroom's best work: a

beautiful, occasionally breathtaking, property has been converted into a tremendously user-friendly golf course.

"I've noticed a marked trend in recent years to get more into really enlightened course strategy, emphasizing finesse and course management skills, as opposed to power," McBroom says.

"There is definitely a trend to high-quality design. I don't necessarily mean a high budget or moving great amounts of earth. I mean courses that are very, very well thought out from points of views like quality of the golf experience for all kinds of players, and which place great emphasis on strategy and which aren't tremendously long."

Bell Bay is the epitome of that philosophy, with most holes appearing more

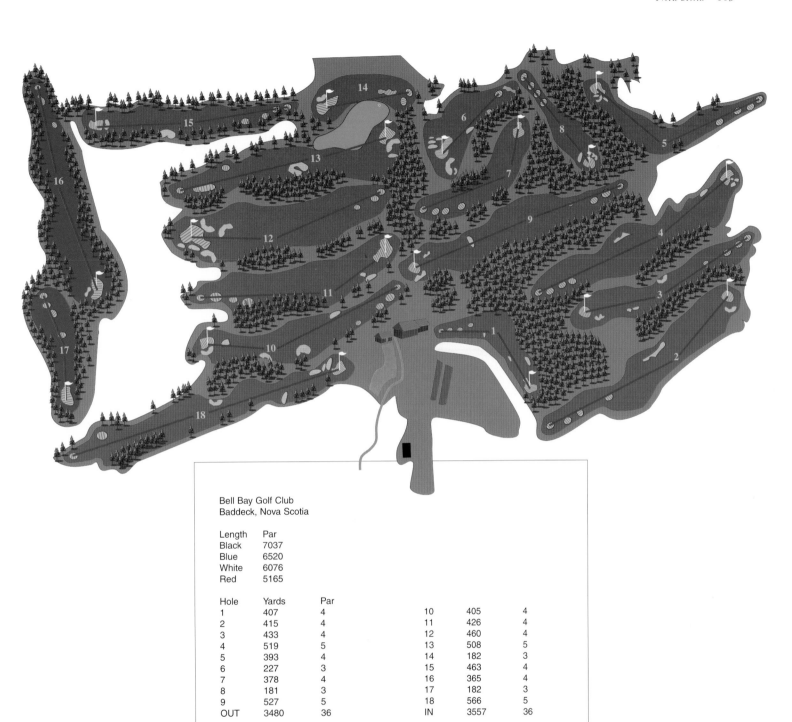

Bell Bay Golf Club
Baddeck, Nova Scotia

Length	Par
Black	7037
Blue	6520
White	6076
Red	5165

Hole	Yards	Par			
1	407	4	10	405	4
2	415	4	11	426	4
3	433	4	12	460	4
4	519	5	13	508	5
5	393	4	14	182	3
6	227	3	15	463	4
7	378	4	16	365	4
8	181	3	17	182	3
9	527	5	18	566	5
OUT	3480	36	IN	3557	36
			Total	7037	72

The new Bell Bay Golf Course, in the quaint village of Baddeck on Nova Scotia's Cape Breton Island, joins another of Canada's great golf courses – Highlands Links — in making Eastern Canada a legitimate golf destination. Overlooking Great Bras D'Or Lake, golfers at Bell Bay can gaze across the water at vintage sailing ships and the baronial home of telephone inventor Alexander Graham Bell. At Bell Bay, history joins with modern course design to provide a terrific memory.

The 17th hole is a great par 3 both visually and strategically. Carry the crevasse and err to the left, if at all.

difficult than they are. Granted, the course stretches just over 7,000 yards and even the Canadian Tour pros had a tough time from the tips when they visited in 1998. Select the right tees for your ability and you are assured of a wonderful outing.

Terraced into a hillside, Bell Bay reposes across Bras D'Or Lake, the world's largest saltwater lake, from Alexander Graham Bell's summer mansion. Just down the road is the quaint tourist village of Baddeck, with craft shops, inns and cafes. Appropriate to its subdued environs, the course sits calmly on the land; both it and its modest but extremely well-appointed clubhouse prefer to impress with quiet quality, not boisterous bravado. The overall impression is one of serenity.

The course yardage guide, cleverly titled "The Navigator," carries the maritime theme throughout. Each hole is named after a ship built in the local boatyards. The No. 1 handicap hole, "Scrapper," commemorates a ship built at Alexander Graham Bell's laboratories. And a scrappy hole this is. Two mighty blows are required to reach

the green that awaits some 433 yards from the tee, especially with an uphill approach into the teeth of the prevailing wind.

The layout is cunningly designed to build to a crescendo, culminating in the final four holes. This is not to say the previous 14 are less than splendid, but rather that the trademark of Bell Bay is that it finishes with a flourish.

"The finish starts with the demanding 470-yard, par-4 15th hole, which demands a big second shot to a green set below the level of the fairway in a wooded hillside," says McBroom. "The 16th plays through a densely wooded fissure and although short, requires exact precision both in the tee shot and in the second.

"The 17th, a mid-length par 3, plays across a wooded creek valley and is one of the most exciting par 3s you will ever play. The 18th is a big three-shot par 5 with a spectacular view of the village of Baddeck and the Bras D'Or Lake. The hole returns slightly uphill across a great gorge on the tee shot and winds back up the hill to the clubhouse, looming on the horizon beyond the green."

Bell Bay is an example of how a talented architect explores the breadth of his abilities. It is a testament to owners Sandy Campbell, Scott MacAulay, Carlyle Chow, and Bruce Anderson, who survived naysayers and even hurricanes to bring their dream to fruition. It is a milestone in Nova Scotia's quest to make rugged Cape Breton Island an international golf destination.

Bell Bay is a jewel set among the ancient forest overlooking Cape Breton Island's rocky crags and lakes.

Known locally as "Killer," the long and narrow seventh hole is the toughest test at Highlands Links on Cape Breton Island.

——— Ingonish Beach, Nova Scotia ———

——— Ingonish Beach, Nova Scotia ———

HIGHLANDS LINKS

Cape Breton Highlands National Park

Architect: Stanley Thompson
Head Professional: Joe Robinson
Superintendent: Martin Walsh

"This is the Cypress Point of Canada for sheer beauty," the late George Knudson once labelled Highlands Links. "When you're driving up the road to the course, it's like driving up to heaven."

Emerging from the fog which often enshrouds the top of Smoky Mountain, the highest point in Nova Scotia near the outermost tip of Cape Breton Island, awaits a heavenly golf experience indeed. For there, carved out of virgin forest 50 years ago, rests a rugged giant called Highlands Links.

When Stanley Thompson trekked to the wilds of Cape Breton at the invitation of the federal government, to build a course within the confines of Cape Breton Highlands National Park, he discovered a challenge appropriate for the man who constructed such wilderness gems as Banff Springs and Jasper Park.

"Stanley Thompson in his early days sometimes would use little more than instinct in laying out his courses . . . striving to retain as much of the natural ground formation as possible. The most beautiful courses, he is convinced — the ones where the greens invite your shots — are the ones which hew most closely to nature," John La Cerda wrote in the Saturday Evening Post in 1946. Highlands Links, like his glorious Capilano on Canada's western coast in West Vancouver, demonstrates the genius of Thompson's instinct.

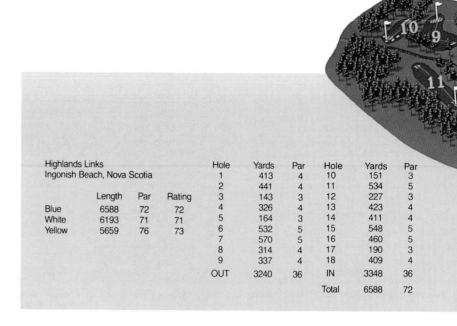

Highlands Links Ingonish Beach, Nova Scotia				Hole	Yards	Par	Hole	Yards	Par
				1	413	4	10	151	3
				2	441	4	11	534	5
	Length	Par	Rating	3	143	3	12	227	3
Blue	6588	72	72	4	326	4	13	423	4
White	6193	71	71	5	164	3	14	411	4
Yellow	5659	76	73	6	532	5	15	548	5
				7	570	5	16	460	5
				8	314	4	17	190	3
				9	337	4	18	409	4
				OUT	3240	36	IN	3348	36
							Total	6588	72

Like all the par-threes at Highlands Links, the 10th hole is pretty, but tough.

Here, in the shadow of Mount Franey, within sight of the Atlantic Ocean and the Clyburn River, using manual labor and horsedrawn implements, Thompson created a masterpiece. It does not overpower with length (the course plays less than 6,600 yards from the tips), but rather with relentless demands on the golfer to produce the exact shot required.

Although the actual golf holes are not lengthy by modern standards, be prepared for a vigorous outing. The links-style course (nine holes out from the clubhouse and nine back) loops around an 11-kilometre routing. A walk from one green to the next tee may cover 300 metres or more, but the flora, fauna and spectacular scenery make the exertion worthwhile. Golf carts are not available. "Take a box lunch out there, go out for 18 holes and you're gone for the day," Knudson advised.

On most holes, a level lie is the only reward for a perfectly placed shot; on some, the teeing ground offers the only flat surface. During construction, huge boulders were tumbled onto the fairways, covered with topsoil and seed, and have become massive moguls to be negotiated with extreme care. The greens, as inviting as Thompson may have intended them, are characterized by swales running through the surface and flanked by sand traps.

After negotiating the first hole, a 408-yard

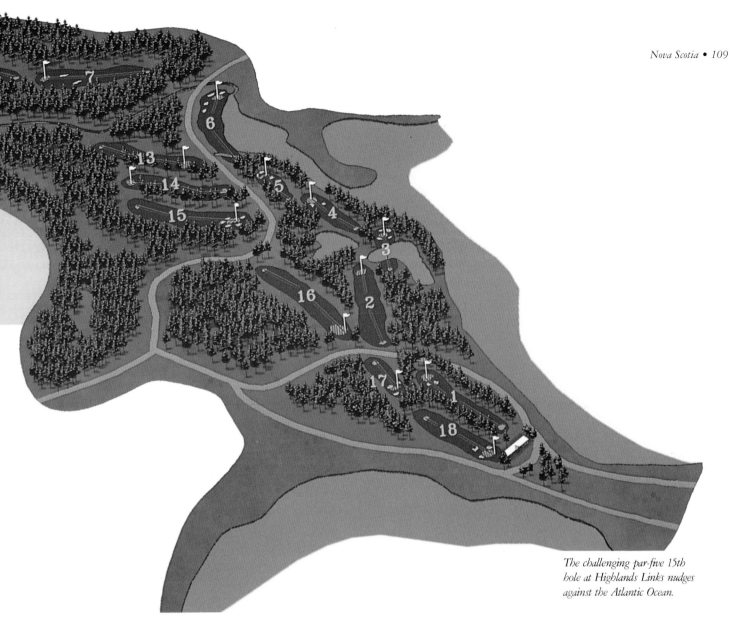

The challenging par-five 15th hole at Highlands Links nudges against the Atlantic Ocean.

par-four, you look back at the modest club-house, and beyond in stark contrast to the deep green forest covering Mount Franey, sits Keltic Lodge. With its white clapboard and red tile roof, the quaint, comfortable lodge (world-renowned for its lobster dinners) is only a few hundred metres from the course.

All the holes bear Gaelic names, as befits a course called Highlands Links. Some are humorous ("Muckle Mouth Meg"), others puzzling ("Tattie Bogle" translates as "potato pits"), but few are as appropriate as that affixed to the fourth hole: Heich O'Fash (Heap of Trouble).

Rated as the Number 1 stroke hole, the 270-yard 4th (Heich O' Fash) deceives the unwary or the over-confident player with its lack of length. An accurate tee shot will attain the top of a plateau which rises from the fairway about 150 yards out. Approach shots to the green, situated on a second plateau, must take into account the ugly fact that inaccuracy will be punished severely. Being left or right could mean a lost ball, while the cunningly sloped green may reject a less-than-perfect attempt and spit it into the trees and tangled

rough which surround the putting surface.

One of Thompson's trademarks, fairway bunkers some 30 yards short of the green, provide another unwelcome surprise on the fourth hole. First-time players may assume these bunkers are green-side and find themselves two or three clubs short on their approach. After surviving Heich O'Fash, glance right to see another emblem of Highlands Links' uniqueness: lobster dories tied up where the river juts into the adjacent fairway.

The seventh hole is called Killiecrankie, which translates as "a long and narrow pass," but perhaps the local nickname, "Killer," reveals more about its character. A 556-yard par-five, the seventh is rated the toughest hole on the course. Bounded by majestic maples, the narrow double-dogleg defends itself admirably from those long hitters who try to reach the green in two. Its defences include Highlands Links' ever-present uneven lies, and a huge bunker guarding the right side of the green. Your task is far from complete once on the

putting surface: a long, two-tiered green offers a myriad of pin locations.

On Number 15 (Tattie Bogle), the ideal tee shot requires a powerful blow over the hill on the left. The third shot on this 546-yard par-five is to a green, surrounded by five bunkers, which sits almost at the front doorstep of St. Paul's Church. First-time visitors are sometimes seen wandering through the adjacent graveyard, pulling golf carts, trying to find the 16th tee.

You may want to take a cue from some of the locals, who dip their golf balls into the holy water at St. Paul's on the way to Number 16. Aptly named Sair Fecht (Hard Work), this relatively short par-five is merciless, but a fantastic golf hole nonetheless. The opening drive on this 458-yarder must carry a ravine or it's "three from the tee." Only a slightly better fate awaits those who hit it straight, for the fairway undulations resemble the surface of the neighboring Atlantic during a winter storm. Picture a herd of buried elephants

---

One of the many unusual aspects of Highlands Links is the Gaelic names given to each hole. Some relate to an aspect of the hole, others were selected simply because of their colorful Scottish flavor. Photograph is of hole number 15, Tattie Bogle.

1. BEN FRANEY: Playing through this fairway presents a full view of Ben Franey. "Ben" is Scottish for "mountain."
2. TAM O'SHANTER: A Scot's bonnet is known as a Tam O'Shanter; in this case, the shape of the green is the reason for the appelation.
3. LOCHAN: A small sheet of water, or miniature lake.
4. HEICH O'FASH: Heap of trouble.
5. CANNY SLAP: A small opening, or "slap", in a hedge or fence.
6. MUCKLE MOUTH MEG: Reportedly, Muckle Mouth Meg, a Scottish lass from Hawick, could swallow a whole "Bubbly Jock's Egg" (a turkey egg).
7. KILLERCRANKIE: A long, narrow pass.
8. CABER'S TOSS: The follow-through after tossing the caber (a log used during Highland games) can be described as "up and over."
9. CORBIE'S NEST: A corbie is a crow, while "nest" is high ground.
10. CUDDY'S LUGS: Donkey's ears. A description of the green.
11. BONNIE BURN: A pleasant stream.

12. CLEUGH: Cleugh is a term used for placenames in the Cheviot hills of Scotland. It means a deep gully or ravine with precipitous sides.
13. LAIRD: A Scottish land owner.
14. HAUGH: A small hollow or valley.
15. TATTIE BOGLE: Potato pits. Potatoes are placed in pits and covered with thatch.
16. SAIR FECHT: Hard work.
17. DOWIE DEN: The Scottish border ballad "The Dowie Dens of Yarrow" relates to a massacre.
18. HAME NOO: Home now.

trooping down the fairway and you have a fairly accurate idea of the lie you face.

Parks Canada has been criticized for not contributing enough money to adequately maintain this national treasure, but that situation appears to be improving. Highlands Links hired its first professionally trained course superintendent in 1990, and improvements are noticeable already. This is a golf experience that, regretably, few Canadians have savored. It is guaranteed not to disappoint.

Members of other distinguished golf clubs in Atlantic Canada call Highlands Links "the best course in the world." After delighting in the wild, ethereal beauty of this unique links layout, you may be inclined to agree.

The swales and humps on the 14th hole are typical of the Stanley Thompson layout.

Angus Glen is representative of a new breed of public-access course in Canada, featuring superb service, excellent conditioning and, above all, a great layout. Good news for golfers: A second 18 is in the works.

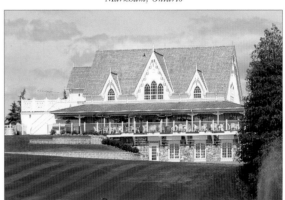

ANGUS GLEN

Golf Club

Public

In 1957, the late Arthur Stollery bought property at the corner of Kennedy Road and Major Mackenzie Drive north of Toronto where he began breeding champion Aberdeen Angus cattle. He named the property, which eventually grew to 800 acres and became his home, Angus Glen Farm. In 1967, he began breeding thoroughbred race horses and, for more than two decades, horses bred at Angus Glen have achieved racing success both in Canada and internationally, including 12 stakes winners, most notably Talkin Man, Kennedy Road and Laurie's Dancer.

After years of touring around his farmlands, Stollery, an avid golfer, began building a golf course in 1992 on some of the original horse paddocks and in the valley where the Angus cattle formerly grazed. Parts of the original farm, which still operates, can be seen adjacent to many of the golf holes. Stollery died in 1994, but his family completed the master-

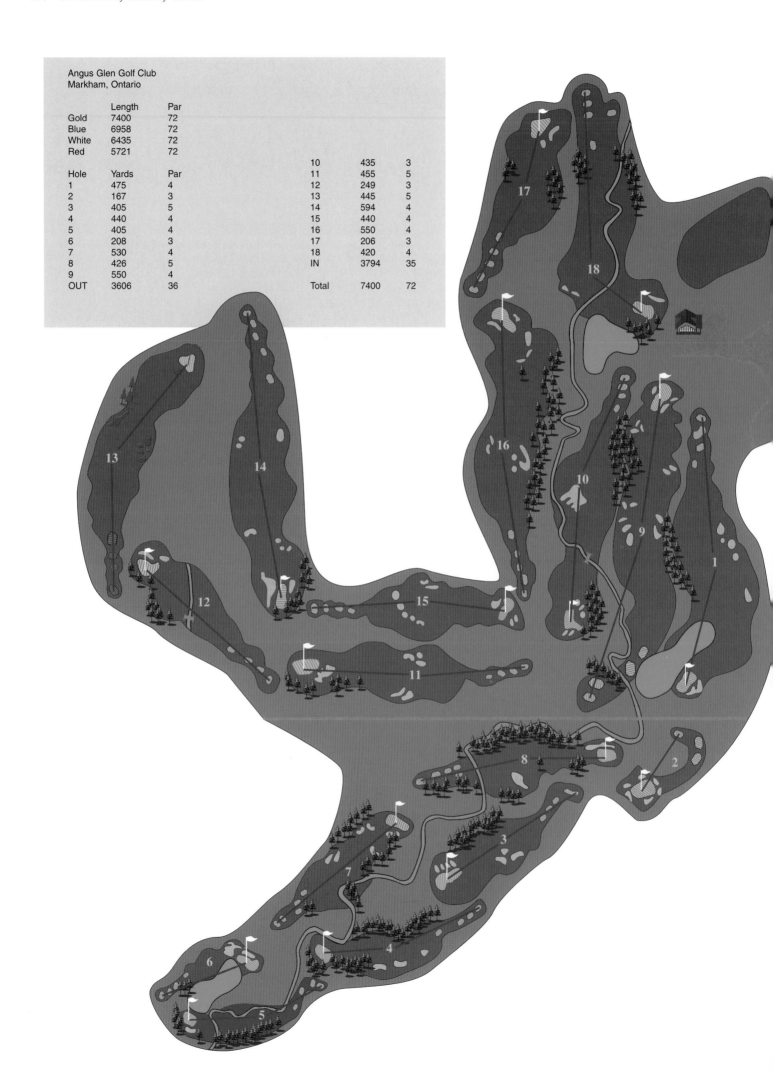

Angus Glen Golf Club
Markham, Ontario

	Length	Par
Gold	7400	72
Blue	6958	72
White	6435	72
Red	5721	72

Hole	Yards	Par
1	475	4
2	167	3
3	405	5
4	440	4
5	405	4
6	208	3
7	530	4
8	426	5
9	550	4
OUT	3606	36

Hole	Yards	Par
10	435	3
11	455	5
12	249	3
13	445	5
14	594	4
15	440	4
16	550	4
17	206	3
18	420	4
IN	3794	35
Total	7400	72

piece which opened to the public in 1995. That year, *Golf Digest* ranked Angus Glen Golf Club as the best new course in Canada.

Designed by Doug Carrick of Toronto, the first 18 holes were designed around native vegetation and feature natural valley holes as well as open, rolling terrain, with the Bruce Creek meandering throughout. In addition to an expansive housing development, an additional 18 holes, designed by Carrick and Jay Morrish, will be added in 1999.

The first hole at Angus Glen sets the bar quite high if you are intent on posting one of your better scores. The fairway slopes from right to left, with a large pond threatening the approach to the green. The ideal tee shot will carry the left fairway bunkers. Avoiding both the pond on the right and a greenside bunker on the left may allow you to eke out a par. At 167 yards from the back tees, the second hole is the shortest hole at Angus Glen, but four bunkers in front of the green and two more behind make it no weak sister. Being short or right is anathema.

Risk or reward? The perfect tee shot on the 405-yard, par-4 third hole must fly the fairway bunkers to set up a short-iron approach to a tough green. A large grassy hollow and four bunkers guard the putting surface. The fifth hole puzzles most first-timers but a long fade past the corner of the dogleg sets up the best approach to a pretty but devilish green site wedged between a grove of cedars and Bruce Creek, some 25 feet below the level of the fairway.

No. 5 may be the most demanding driving hole on the course. A good smack down the right, flirting with the creek, will open up the most opportune approach for avoiding the pond on the right. The sixth, a 208-yard par 3, is as picturesque as it is difficult. Club selection is important if you intend on getting the ball close to the hole on this long, shallow, and undulating green.

The par-5 seventh hole plays from an elevated tee which allows you to view the entire hole. Two long and accurate shots will have you putting for eagle on this small green. Good luck! On the eighth, a towering white pine on the right side of

The prevailing wind adds yet another difficulty factor to the 455-yard, par-4 11th. Avoid the particularly deep bunkers at all cost.

The 435-yard 10th hole features a huge bunker shaped like a dinosaur's foot and marshy hazard which threaten errant tee shots. The approach is to a greatly elevated green. A tough par-4.

the fairway can stymie a misdirected tee shot. A shallow fade which avoids the tree will leave a mid- to short-iron approach. The tee shot from the tips on the par-5 ninth hole is one of the highlights at Angus Glen. A long draw will carry the five bunkers flanking the fairway on the left and then roll as much as 30 yards, setting up an opportunity to go for the green in two.

Although only 435 yards from the championship tees, the 10th hole presents a strategic and physical challenge to any player. A marshy waste area bisects the fairway, threatening an overly long tee shot. A perfectly played drive will leave a mid-iron into this elevated, dual-level green protected by three deep bunkers. But leave nothing in the bag on 11, a long par 4 usually played into the wind, or on 12 — a par 3 measuring almost 250 yards, again into the prevailing wind. Cut the dogleg on No. 13 to hit the downhill slope and gain extra yards of roll, allowing a much shorter approach shot. The architect had some fun with 14, a long par 5 where the spacious rolling fairway weaves

back and forth between nine bunkers, allowing for many strategic options.

The closing holes commence with 15, a par 4 featuring crossbunkers that angle from left to right. The par-5 16th calls for a long tee shot down the left side to achieve the best angle to the terraced second landing area. The penultimate hole, modeled after the famous Redan at Scotland's North Berwick West Links, is a par 3 angled from left to right. A high soft fade is the answer to a back right pin. At all costs, avoid the two bunkers fronting the green — they are the deepest at Angus Glen. The final hole, a pretty but dangerous par 4 of 420 yards, calls for an accurate tee shot as close as you dare to the creek on the left to optimize the approach shot.

Right from its opening day, when it was recognized as the best new course in the country, Angus Glen has epitomized great golf and sterling service. Under the direction of the Stollery family and the guidance of general manager Kevin Thistle, the facility continues to set new standards within the industry. Best of all, it's open to the public.

Angus Glen: Very few courses have the audacity to make the opening hole the toughest. That's right: the first hole at Angus Glen is the No. 1 handicap hole. While the architectural merits of this can be argued, it does alert the first-time guest that this is not your ordinary public golf course. It's also a stiff reminder to keep the excellent yardage guide close at hand. For the neophyte, the best placement of your drive is over the left fairway bunkers. Then you are confronted with a precision shot to a green flanked by water and sand. Good luck.

The 208-yard sixth hole: This long par 3 plays from an elevated tee to a long, shallow, and undulating green.

The 400-yard 13th hole signals the start of Beacon Hall's toughest stretch.

BEACON HALL

Golf and Country Club

Architect: Bob Cupp with Thomas McBroom
Head Professional: Phil Hardy
Manager: Gary Carl

Beacon Hall has been called "the most exclusive golf club in Canada," and it may well be in terms of number of members. A mere 230 purists belong to this classically understated refuge built on a magnificent site north of Toronto. Indeed, only a handful of golf clubs in North America have a smaller membership roster. Membership at Beacon Hall is not something one brags about, but it is something to be very proud of — the course was ranked fifth in the country by SCORE, the national golf magazine, in its first year of eligibilty in 1990.

From the back tees, Beacon Hall approaches 7,000 yards, "a course for players of supreme ability," says course architect Bob Cupp, himself a former PGA Tour pro. "Though they are few, they do have a tremendous influence over the reputation of the course." Cupp says that while the course could host any tournament from a stategic point of view, due to the underlying philosophy of the wealthy members to shun publicity, "there will be no accommodations for gallery or tournament operations. This is a course for the members — but with enough teeth to gain the respect of even the severest critics." This is not to say that Cupp's design excludes players of lesser ability: "The members' course will be

all of the members' course," he says, and it is true that the other tee postions offer a gratifying, yet challenging, test.

The very existence of Beacon Hall is gratifying as well to those few individuals who, concerned about crowded conditions at other Toronto private clubs, decided to assemble a group to purchase the former Toronto and North York Hunt Club and an adjacent farm to give Cupp the land he needed to create a "world-class" facility. As well, 80 attractive, expensive and unobtrusive housing units were planned: their sale would provide true aficionados with a residence on one of the country's finest course and assist with the project's financing. Cupp was impressed by the group's efforts, calling the 260 acres the best piece of property he had ever had the opportunity to work with. The result, which opened in 1988, is a golfer's dream: a masterful routing taking full advantage of the property's varying personalties. "Every shot will be presented like

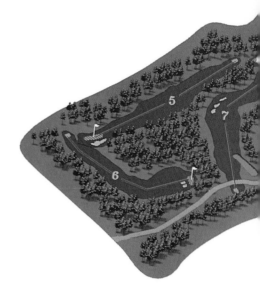

The third hole at Beacon Hall winds through pines reminiscent of the Carolinas.

Beacon Hall Golf Club Aurora, Ontario			
	Length	Par	Rating
Blue	6907	72	74.5
White	6251	72	71
Yellow	5247	72	66
Hole	Yards	Par	
1	360	4	
2	367	4	
3	202	3	
4	587	5	
5	429	4	
6	358	4	
7	550	5	
8	167	3	
9	400	4	
OUT	3420	36	
10	576	5	
11	162	3	
12	496	5	
13	404	4	
14	201	3	
15	593	5	
16	226	3	
17	406	4	
18	446	4	
IN	3514	36	
Total	6934	72	

a picture," Cupp resolved when designing the course, and he delivered on that promise.

The first four holes play through towering red pines reminiscent of the Carolinas, and then the vegetation makes a pleasing switch to burly hardwoods — maples, oaks and walnuts. The back nine, with its mammoth sand hill and swales swathed in native grasses, takes the player on an imaginary and tactical visit to the links courses of Scotland and Ireland. The finishing hole unites the features in summary; looking back off the tee, adjacent to the first green and its protective pines, your eyes pan across the sandy mounds of the back nine, but your drive must carry uphill through more hardwoods.

"I think Bob Cupp designed the course beautifully," says Head Professional Phil Hardy. "The first six holes combine a gentle invitation to the course with a taste of what's to come. The next six say, 'Here's where you make your move,' with their three par-fives. The final six are all golf. They've killed a lot of hopes. I've seen great players come to 15, 16, 17 or 18 at- or under-par and walk off the course without finishing."

That last stretch obviously is key to a good round at Beacon Hall. It commences with Number 13, a 400-yard par-four with a generous fairway, inviting the player to "bust it," says Cupp. As on many of the holes, the fairway bunkers — on the left in this case — indicate the best postion. "At this course, the fairway bunkers are usually saying, 'Come as close to me as you dare,'" says Hardy. "They indicate where you have the best approach, where you will have the most green to work with." On 13, you are penalized if you don't flirt with these traps: an approach from anywhere else must carry over a particularly nasty greenside bunker.

The next hole plays 199 yards from the back tees. This claustrophic par-three is hemmed in on three sides by mounds or hills. The green is guarded by two bunkers, one of which is three metres deep. If you are playing the white tees, play safe to the left and bounce the ball onto the green, advises Cupp.

The par-five 15th hole presents a heroic challenge from the tee. Its split fairway is separated by a waste bunker the size of a football field — one acre in area. The short, or left, route requires precision to place the ball in a landing area only 30 yards wide, but offers

The 18th hole at Beacon Hall rises toward the clubhouse.

the successful gambler a long-iron approach to a severely contoured green guarded by three bunkers on the right. The player who elects to stay right and hope for par must follow Cupp's prescription: A drive to the corner of the dogleg, a long-iron or fairway wood near a bunker set in a mogul on the right side and then a wedge to cover the remaining 80 or 90 yards to the two-tiered green.

"If there is a supreme test at Beacon Hall, this is it," says Cupp about the par-three 16th, and everyone who has played the course agrees with him. At 228 yards from the blue tees and 213 from the whites, this hole may require more club than some players have in their bags, especially if played into the wind. The intervening area between the elevated tee and green is layered in tall, waving fescue grass

and swallows any errant shot, although there is a landing area left of the green.

The 17th hole, a straightaway par-four, reiterates one of the underlying design principles at Beacon Hall: play as close as you can to the fairway bunkers on the right because the green opens up fully from that side. Being in the left greenside bunker means playing out of the sand directly toward a pond — not a desireable scenario.

As mentioned, the finishing hole combines all the esthetic qualities of the property, but it also presents the final strategic challenge of the round. A good drive on this lengthy par-four (448 from the blues, 409 from the whites) will be followed by a long-iron toward the well-mounded and - bunkered green near the clubhouse.

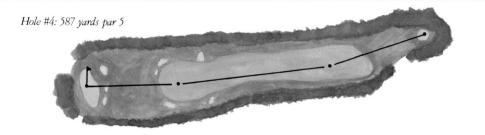

Hole #4: 587 yards par 5

The Toughest Hole at Beacon Hall

The 587-yard fourth hole, the first par-five encountered at Beacon Hall, is rated the most difficult hole on the course. In the words of course designer Bob Cupp, "The drive will be played from an elevated tee across a depression to a fairway rising and winding to the right. The tee shot from the white and yellow markers will be substantially farther forward, but uphill. Once the players successfully reaches the first landing area, the next challenge is reaching the second landing area and 'setting up' the approach. The second landing area is actually in the shape of a giant green, nearly 47,000 square feet — about an acre — and a fair challenge for the three-wood or long-iron required to get there. From anywhere on the second landing area, the green will be visible and a fair target. The shot to the green will be the first true test of the round. The putting surface lies at the top of a rise. Three bunkers rest in the front slope of the green area. The back is supported by low mounds. Anything over the green will roll down the backslope; a formidable hazard."

The greens at Beacon Hall are straightforward; the challenge is to get to them in regulation.

Number 15 demands a 240-yard carry to reach the fairway from the back tees.

BLUE SPRINGS
Golf Club

Architect: Don Dawkins
Director of Golf Operations: Craig Guthrie
Head Professional: Shelley Woolner
Superintendent: Ted Ellis

"Unique" may be an overworked term when it comes to golf courses, but it is appropriate when applied to Blue Springs Golf Club near Guelph.

Built on a 540-acre site with dramatic elevation changes, 23 ponds and stands of mature forest, Blue Springs is the brainchild of Don Dawkins, founder of the Olde Hide House. The slogan of the Olde Hide House, a retailer of leather furniture and apparel, is "it's worth the drive to Acton." Dawkins' latest venture makes that doubly true.

Dawkins and his partners have used their marketing genius to put the name of Blue Springs on many golfers' lips, nationally as well as locally. One of their first moves was to negotiate a deal with the Canadian Professional Golfers' Association to build its headquarters there. As part of the agreement, Blue Springs will play host to one of the CPGA's national championships every year. "The move made sense for us because of the good management and the outstanding golf course," says CPGA Executive Director Dave Colling.

The next move was to develop a teaching program in which head pro Shelley Woolner and Ben Kern from the National Golf

The par-5 12th yeilds may more double bogeys than birdies.

Blue Springs Golf Club
Acton, Ontario

	Length	Par	Rating
Gold	6715	72	73.5
Blue	6406	72	71.9
White	6106	72	70.4
Red	5188	72	65.8

Hole	Yards	Par
1	373	4
2	217	3
3	330	4
4	524	5
5	183	3
6	366	4
7	421	4
8	392	4
9	485	5
OUT	3291	36
10	425	4
11	156	3
12	515	5
13	384	4
14	451	4
15	512	5
16	386	4
17	177	3
18	423	4
IN	3424	36
Total	6715	72

Club offer instruction packages ranging from an hour to a week at Blue Springs' great facilites.

The membership concept combines the best of both worlds. While Blue Springs is open to the public, a small number of transferable memberships is available, offering advanced booking of tee times, unrestricted use of various facilities and virtually unlimited play on the Turtle Lake and Trillium courses. That's right — Dawkins and his group had the foresight to build not one, but two layouts.

The Turtle Lake course is a 6,700-yard test while the Trillium is a nine-hole, par-3 track ideal for beginners, juniors and seniors. "Unique" may be applied to the way they were created.

In 1987, Dawkins says, "we had an Olde Hide House management meeting and the decision was made to diversify. Golf and real estate were the first options that came up and within a year of that discussion we bought the property to develop that idea."

The final result covered both goals. In addition to the golf component, there are 40 estate lots of between one and three acres overlooking the courses.

Dawkins, the nominal architect, says everyone on the management committee, "whether their handicap was five or 35," had input into the design of the course. Hole design was continually in flux, even during the building stages, with par 3s being changed to par 4s, and so on. "Our affiliation with the CPGA meant we had to go for quality," Dawkins says. "During construction we redesigned four holes. We didn't hesitate to evaluate what we were doing while we were doing it. We did this more as a work of art than an engineering project."

While the staggering elevation changes make a cart all but a necessity, the Turtle Lake course reflects its democratic origins by offering an enjoyable experience for golfers of all skill levels. Four sets of tees mean the length of the course can vary from 6,715 yards to 5,188. Every aspect of a player's game is examined during a round here, especially putting.

Several holes merit special attention, in-

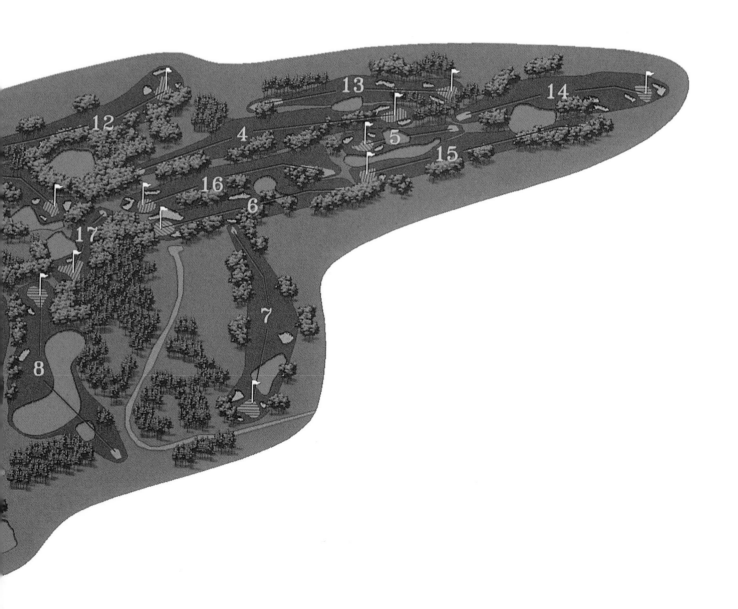

The Eighth Hole at Blue Springs

The eighth hole has been identified as one of the signature holes at Blue Springs — although the course has been called "a collection of signature holes" — and it may be the toughest. The drive originates from an elevated tee set back in a chute of trees, and it must carry a large pond to a generous landing area with a large fairway bunker. It is a classic challenge of the "risk-reward" school of design. The more you cut across the pond, the shorter your approach shot is. The second shot into an sloping, narrow green must thread the needle between woods on the right and a bunker on the front left.

Many call the 17th Blue Springs' "signature hole."

An elevated tee, water and rock make the 10th a dramatic hole.

cluding the second, eighth (see sidebar), the 10th, 14th and 17th.

The par-3 second hole stretches to 217 yards from the back tees and, if the wind is blowing, is a stern test. Adding to the difficulty is a large bunker on the front left and four pot bunkers behind. The tee is elevated with the large sloping green set in the valley below. "The hole was set up with two very difficult pin placements," say the designers. "The back right means the golfer must contend with the traps, while a back left position means using a wood off the tee."

The 10th has been called "one of the most dramatic holes at Blue Springs." A 425-yard par 4, the hole plays to a green almost 100 yards below the teeing ground. Length off the tee is not critical, but accuracy on the second shot is. An elevated green is surrounded by a pond, bunkers and bush on the back and left. The hole is visually striking, with natural rock forming a backdrop to the pond. "The backbone of a golf course is the long par 4" say the

designers, "and this is it on Blue Springs."

The 14th is a 450-yard dogleg right and the longest of the par 4s. You don't normally get a break from the wind on this hole; it's usually in your face as you stand on the tee. Five tee blocks add to the flexibility if the wind is too strong. The front tees are some 130 yards closer to the pin. A 200 foot long trap engulfs the right side of the fairway, forcing golfers to stay left, and then large traps surround the green, making an accurate long-iron shot a must. Things don't get any easier once you get to the green, which slopes from back to front."

The 17th is notable not necessarily because of its difficulty but because of its beauty. Its length varies from 177 from the golds to 136 at the forward tees, allowing every player to enjoy its attributes. Played from the top of a cliff some 80 feet above the green over a pond and small waterfall to a large sloping green framed by trees, the 17th is a memorable hole. From the championship tees, 10 holes are clearly visible.

Ottawa, Ontario

CAMELOT

Golf and Country Club

Architect: Thomas McBroom
General Manager: Don Noseworthy
Head Professional: Barry Laphen
Superintendent: Robin Stafford

"God himself put this piece of land here for a golf course," says Camelot co-founder Don Noseworthy. And it is with near-religious fervor that Noseworthy preaches the merits of this magnificent layout just east of Canada's capital city.

Obviously, Noseworthy is not alone in his lofty estimation of Camelot. In 1993, the course was selected as runnerup by the U.S. publication Golf Digest in the category "best new private course in Canada," and anyone fortunate enough to play it will not question the judges' decision which is based on the criteria of shot values, playability, design balance, memorability and aesthetics.

Overlooking the mighty Ottawa River, Camelot offers a vast variety of aesthetic and golfing pleasures. Nature did its part by providing stands of ancient pines, rippling lakes, significant elevation changes and precipitous ravines.

"It's a gorgeous site," agrees course architect Tom McBroom of Toronto. "It's half woods and half open, situated on a high ridge overlooking the Ottawa River. From the clubhouse, you can see 30 miles down the river as well as overlooking nine

holes of the golf course. It's a really dramatic property punctuated by steep wooded slopes. The site offers spectacular elevated tee shots.

"Camelot is really a combination of two characteristics. It's links-style up top in the meadowland where the holes are defined by the fescue roughs. The rest is situated in a woodsy parkland. It's a great contrast.

"I think Camelot is important in a number of ways," says the architect, "not the least of which is that it is the first significant addition to the Ottawa Valley golf scene in decades; since the opening of Royal Ottawa and Ottawa Hunt."

This "significant addition" is the realized dream of one man — Don Noseworthy. He describes how the vision of Camelot came to him:

"I was returning from Pebble Beach following Tom Watson's dramatic victory over Jack Nicklaus in 1982 when I made the decision to build a golf course. Pebble Beach has always been my favorite place on earth and I am certain that the inspiration to fulfil a life-long dream began amid the wind and the beauty of Pebble Beach.

"The Ottawa River is not the Pacific Ocean," acknowledges the man who became Camelot's first president and general manager, "but the views from the land we chose in 1988 are spectacular.

Noseworthy says other names were considered before settling on Camelot. "Some of the interesting connections between our course and the original Camelot include the fact that King Arthur and his Knights of the Round Table were originally thought to occupy a part of England known as Cumberland. Cumberland is the name of the township where the golf course is located.

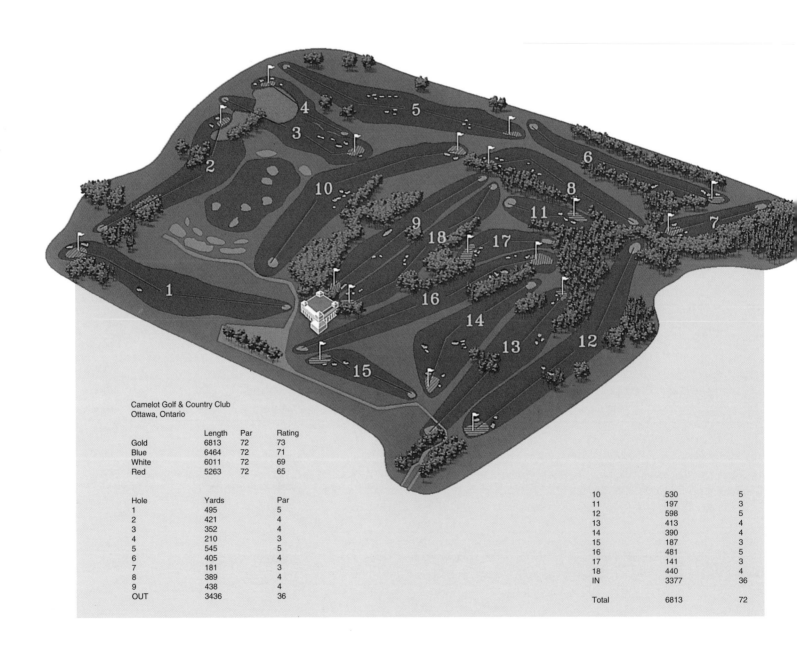

Camelot Golf & Country Club
Ottawa, Ontario

	Length	Par	Rating
Gold	6813	72	73
Blue	6464	72	71
White	6011	72	69
Red	5263	72	65

Hole	Yards	Par
1	495	5
2	421	4
3	352	4
4	210	3
5	545	5
6	405	4
7	181	3
8	389	4
9	438	4
OUT	3436	36

Hole	Yards	Par
10	530	5
11	197	3
12	598	5
13	413	4
14	390	4
15	187	3
16	481	5
17	141	3
18	440	4
IN	3377	36
Total	6813	72

*Cut the dogleg on Number 14
— if you dare.*

"In addition there was a huge stone on the property that was perfect for inserting Excalibur, the magic sword. And the code of ethics of the Knights of the Round Table were not unlike the ethics portion of the Rules of Golf. Besides, as the song says: 'In short, there's simply not a more congenial spot than Camelot.'"

Having found the property and selected the name, Noseworthy entered into a partnership with local businessmen Philippe and Andre Gagnon. "We decided to go the equity route to raise the funds to build our dream," recalls Noseworthy. "I sold my business and became the project manager and salesman. In 1989, we broke ground and selected Thomas McBroom as our architect.

"Tom and I worked well together. We both felt that the land itself should dictate the routing of the course. The course far exceeded our expectations."

The first hole is a short par 5 characterized by a waste bunker that runs down the right side of the fairway. The second or third shot must carry a large gorge and creek to an elevated, well-bunkered green. A canyon-like effect is created by mounds surrounding the perimeter of the hole. Number 2 is one of the most demanding holes at Camelot: the tee shot must carry a creek on the left side of the fairway while the second shot must avoid a large pond on the left. The third requires a tee shot between two large lakes and the par-3 fourth challenges the player to carry part of a lake in front of the large, well-protected green.

Number 5 can only be described as a spectacular par 5. From an elevated tee, the player must choose between two fairways: the shorter route crosses a series of bunkers guarding the left side and the second shot must avoid fairway bunkers lining the ever-narrowing fairway. The tree-line sixth hole

The fourth green is tucked dangerously behind a pond.

plays uphill to a large, open green. An apple orchard is home to the beautiful par-3 seventh hole. The green is perched on the edge of a very steep ravine, so it won't do to be long or left here.

The eighth hole is described as short but treacherous. The tee shot must reach the corner of the dogleg and the second shot must carry a gorge. Number 9 is visually stunning: the tee shot is played from an elevated tee which affords a panoramic view of the countryside. The second shot from the valley floor must carry all the way to the large elevated double green which serves both the ninth and 18th holes.

The back nine commences with a medium-length par 5 which plays into the prevailing wind. The long par-3 11th hole plays downhill across a gorge and Number 12 is the toughest on the course (see sidebar). It is followed by the most challenging par 4 at Camelot. This dogleg left boasts an approach shot played through a chute of trees to an elevated green. Fourteen may be the most interesting par 4 on the course, offering an option: the dogleg left can be cut if the player has the courage and the length to avoid the bunkers on the corner, or you can play to the wide part of the fairway, leaving a mid-iron to the elevated, well-bunkered green.

After the 187-yard par-3 15th hole, you are presented with Number 16 — a great short par 5 presenting three targets that must be hit. The tee shot must be played down the right side and the second shot must be played to the left side to allow for the best view of the green which is on a ledge, surrounded by trouble. The 17th is the shortest hole at Camelot, but compensates for that with a very undulating green. And your round concludes with a classic finishing hole. The 18th is a magnificent par 4, playing from an elevated tee into a beautiful valley and then back up to the spectacular double green.

The Toughest Hole at Camelot
"You have to hit a cannon off this tee in order to be in position to hit the second landing area," says course architect Tom McBroom of the par-5 12th hole at Camelot. "The second shot will be a three-wood or long iron over a rise that is guarded by bunkers. The third shot is a wedge into a tiny green that is bunkered on each side. Length and accuracy are a must. It's not a hole you try to birdie."

The par-3 11th is long but plays downhill across a gorge.

The par-5 14th at Deerhurst Highlands is reachable in two.

DEERHURST HIGHLANDS

Golf Club

Architects:Robert Cupp, Thomas McBroom
Head Professional: Paul Kennedy
Superintendent: Ed Farnsworth

Deerhurst Highlands defines golf in Canada. Winding its majestic way through the ancient forest crowning the craggy Canadian Shield, skirting lakes and streams, this 7,000-yard jewel holds its own with any course in Canada.

Part of the posh four-season Deerhurst Resort (which also boasts an 18-hole, 4,700-yard, par-65 layout in addition to almost every other recreational activity) in the rugged Muskoka region 250 kilometres north of Toronto, the Highlands speaks volumes about the design talents of American Bob Cupp and Toronto's Tom McBroom.

While the strength of the property was based on the unique topography of the Shield, the location also posed many problems, McBroom says. "Deerhurst is built on solid rock. It's comparable in many ways to Banff Springs, which was built in the Rocky Mountains in the 1920s, and was the first course to cost more than $1 million to build. Every cubic inch of topsoil and subsoil had to be brought in." Costruction required the importation of about 15,000 truckloads of sand alone.

Head pro Paul Kennedy calls Deerhurst, which had its first

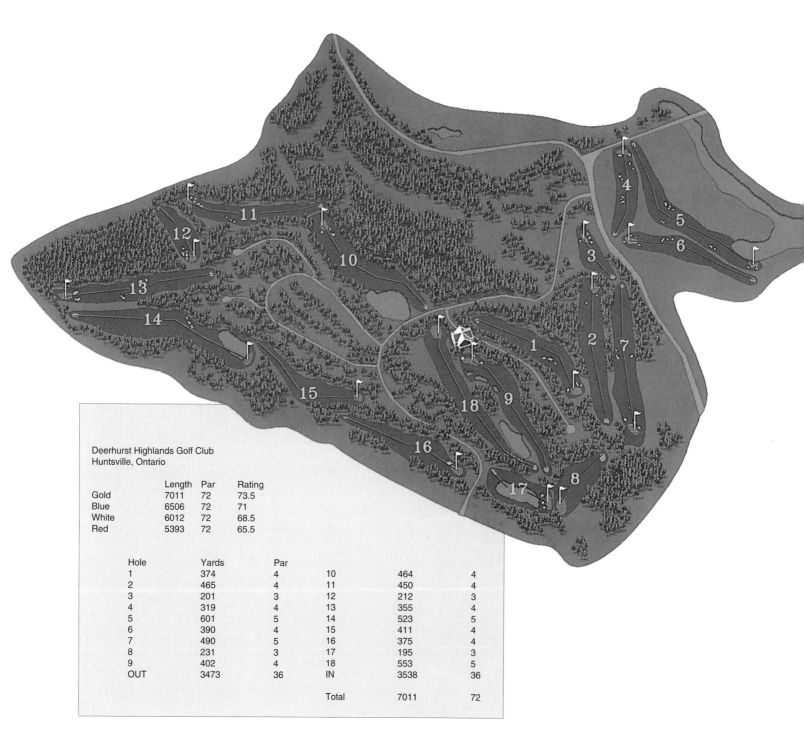

Deerhurst Highlands Golf Club
Huntsville, Ontario

	Length	Par	Rating
Gold	7011	72	73.5
Blue	6506	72	71
White	6012	72	68.5
Red	5393	72	65.5

Hole	Yards	Par				
1	374	4	10		464	4
2	465	4	11		450	4
3	201	3	12		212	3
4	319	4	13		355	4
5	601	5	14		523	5
6	390	4	15		411	4
7	490	5	16		375	4
8	231	3	17		195	3
9	402	4	18		553	5
OUT	3473	36	IN		3538	36
			Total		7011	72

full season in 1991, "a course to challenge the pros and yet, with four different tee blocks, everyone can enjoy it." Kennedy knows whereof he speaks: one of the top pros on the Canadian Tour for years, he won the Canadian Club Pro Championship in 1984 and has been assisting golfers at Deerhurst since 1982.

McBroom also advises visitors (while there is a membership structure, the course is open to the public, although resort guests get a discounted fee) to play the correct tees in order to maximize their enjoyment. "The course is only 6,000 yards from the whites and it's not as intimidating as it looks. We've cleared the fairways extra-wide for the benefit of the occasional golfer and the greens are not severe."

"This is the quintessential Canadian golf course," says the justifiably proud McBroom who previously teamed with Cupp, the design consultant at Augusta National, on the acclaimed Beacon Hall in Aurora, Ontario. Both have impressive individual portfolios as well. "I'm very proud of the way the routing takes advantage of the land. The fit with the natural landscape is strong."

As proof, he cites the second hole, where a straight tee shot is required to clear a sheer 60-foot-high rock face and attain the landing area. But, assures McBroom, "it's not as intimidating as it looks. It's a 185-yard carry from the golds and about 170 from the blues. The trick is to put the visuals out of your mind and swing easy." Despite those reassuring words, the architect calls this hole the most difficult on the course. The second shot is slightly uphill to a green that is not visible, yet the position of the flagstick is obvious. The green, says McBroom, "is large and has three levels. Its saving grace is that it is not bunkered." There are several grassy hollows protecting the putting surface.

The architects say this hole forewarns the player of a concept consistent throughout their design. "At Deerhurst, the rock becomes a major element in the theme of the golf course design. Although never in play, it poses a menacing threat." As McBroom says, disregard the implied threat and swing easy.

The theme reappears on other holes — reinforced with the notations "cliff", "rock" or "boulders" in the course guide — but most notably holes 3, 10 (see sidebar), 12 and 18.

The 12th, a long par 3, features a vertical granite face providing the left backdrop for the green. "The trick is to carry a strategically placed bunker set some 10 yards in front of the green," say the architects. "This bunker will create the illusion of making the putting surface appear closer than it really is. Club selection is paramount."

On 18, use the massive boulder on the left side of the fairway as your target. "Consistent with the concluding holes at many of the world's great golf courses," the architects say, "the 18th hole at Deerhurst demands a long and well-placed tee shot, preferably drawn

Water, rock and forest — all part of the character of Deerhurst Highlands.

Fade your tee shot on Number 11 for the best approach to its angled green.

into a very slight upslope. Designed so as not to be reachable in two, it may still be possible with the execution of an extraordinary tee shot. The second shot is through a long chute bordered by the ninth fairway to the right and a grassy upslope on the left. Cutting in front of the green is a boulder-strewn creek with a series of pools and waterfalls. The perfect second shot must either carry the creek to the putting surface beyond or be positioned short of it. The putting surface is a mass of beautiful swirling contours and will surrender to only the most skilled of shotmakers."

The course complements one of the finest four-season resorts anywhere. Built in 1896 as a fishing lodge by Englishman Charles Waterhouse, Deerhurst now boasts a 110,000 square-foot state-of-the-art complex housing racquet sports, spa, pro shops, pool, conference room and other amenities. Accommodations are varied and first-class.

Deerhurst Highlands rounds out an impressive roster of properties under the umbrella of Canadian Pacific Hotels and Resorts, the largest single owner and operator of golf courses in Canada. Others include Alberta's Banff Springs and Jasper Park Lodge, Chateau Montebello in Quebec, the Algonquin (St. Andrews By-The-Sea, N.B.) and Chateau Whistler (and its brand-new Robert Trent Jones Jr. course), a couple of hours north of Vancouver.

The Signature Hole at Deerhurst Highlands

A descriptive narrative, written by architects Bob Cupp and Tom McBroom, describes the 10th hole: "Designed by Mother Nature, with a small assist from the architects, this hole is arguably one of the prettiest and most demanding in the world. From tees high atop a rocky ridge, the drive must carry a large lake to a perched landing area. Dominating the view from the tee is a vertical granite wall with fairway below and to the left and virgin woods to the right. The tee shot must be long and straight. Visibility of the putting surface is guaranteed only with a drive of 260 yards from the gold tees. The approach to a complex multi-tiered green is through a nest of cross bunkers."

Pick the right club and aim for the centre of the green on the par-3 8th hole.

Double greens, timber- and sod-walled bunkers, and fescue grasses give the Devil's Paintbrush a distinctively British feel. Here, the second and fifth holes come together.

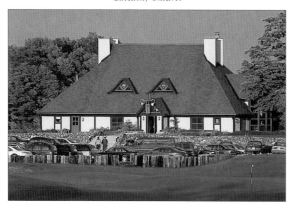

DEVIL'S PAINTBRUSH

Golf Club

Private

On January 7, 1989, a couple of hundred golf nuts mingled in a community centre northwest of Toronto to spend thousands of dollars to join a golf course that existed only on paper. Why the excitement? Because the course was the brainchild of Chris Haney and Scott Abbott — inventors of the wildly successful board game Trivial Pursuit.

The fact that the Devil's Pulpit course (named after a rock formation visible from the course) was many months away from completion did not deter the prospective members. All were banking that Haney and Abbott retained the Midas touch that made them and their Trivial Pursuit investors millionaires.

Those early believers have been proven right many times over — the course, designed by Michael Hurdzan, and the clubhouse are world-class and have received unparalleled acclaim. The crowning touch came when the highly respected U.S. publication *Golf Digest* anointed the Pulpit "the best new

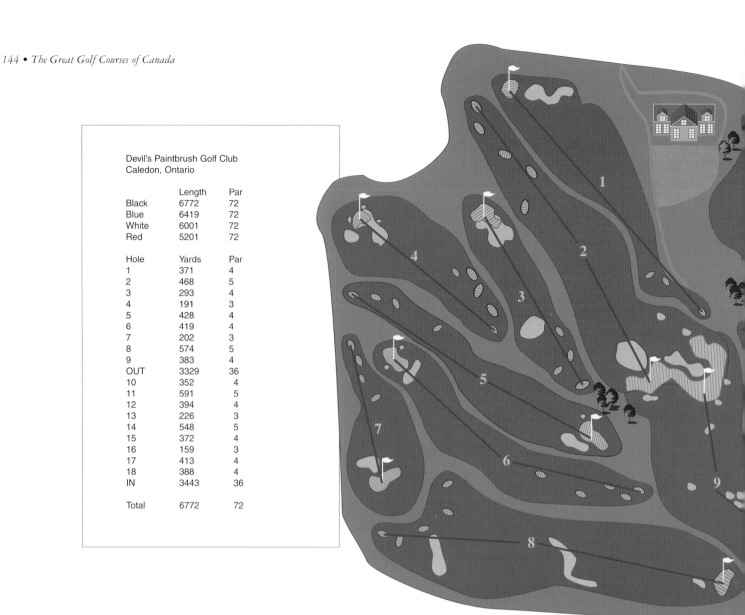

Devil's Paintbrush Golf Club
Caledon, Ontario

	Length	Par
Black	6772	72
Blue	6419	72
White	6001	72
Red	5201	72

Hole	Yards	Par
1	371	4
2	468	5
3	293	4
4	191	3
5	428	4
6	419	4
7	202	3
8	574	5
9	383	4
OUT	3329	36
10	352	4
11	591	5
12	394	4
13	226	3
14	548	5
15	372	4
16	159	3
17	413	4
18	388	4
IN	3443	36
Total	6772	72

The remains of an old barn, stone fences, and true links conditioning belie the Paintbrush's modern origins. This is the eighth hole.

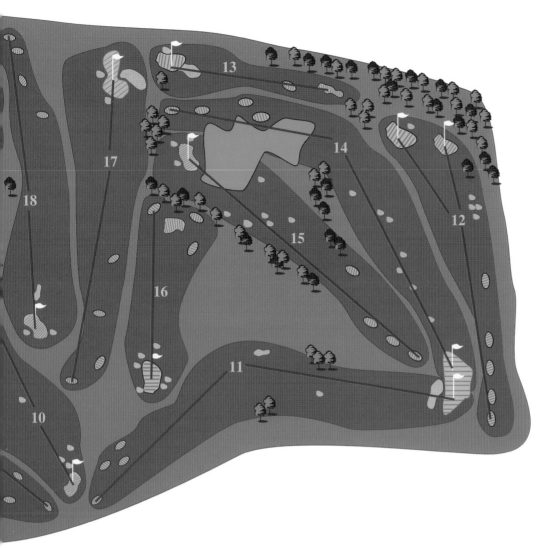

private course in Canada" in 1991.

In an unprecedented "one-two" punch, the Pulpit's sister course, the Devil's Paintbrush, was selected by *Golf Digest* as "best new private course in Canada" in 1992. The two courses combine to create for their extremely fortunate members a golf facility that is unique in the world. Together they form the Devil's Pulpit Golf Association.

The Pulpit, built on 315 acres in the Caledon Hills some 70 kilometres northwest of Toronto, offers a multi-faceted, larger-than-life golf experience that delights the average player and challenges the scratch amateur or pro. Visitors and members alike marvel at its broad, sweeping fairways and extravagant design features, like the par-3 betting hole situated between the two 11th holes. That's right: The Pulpit has 20 holes, although only 18 are played in a given round.

The Paintbrush, located five kilometres away, is a vastly different golf experience. Designed by Hurdzan in a links style, it is "just like Scotland without the North Sea," says Haney. While that may be a touch over the top, anyone fortunate enough to play the 'Brush will forgive Haney his hyperbole.

"This course is as much Ballybunion as Devil's Pulpit is Augusta National," says a course blurb. "The Paintbrush has all of the features of British links courses such as sod- and timber-faced bunkers, treacherous greens, blind shots played over guide rocks, double greens and a constantly moving surface. Almost no place is flat and the entire golf course, except for the greens, is planted in a mixture of fescue grasses."

The Paintbrush, named after a local wildflower, recreates as closely as possible the links golf experienced in Ireland, Scotland, and England. Hurdzan travelled

Deep rough and pot bunkers, like these on the fourth hole, provide as close to a links experience as possible in Ontario. Now if they could just do something about those trees…

to Britain with a Devil's Pulpit delegation before attempting to design the 'Brush. He was especially impressed with Lahinch and Ballybunion in Ireland, and not only with their designs. Recognizing that the conditioning of the golf course was almost as important as the layout to the links golf experience, Hurdzan directed that maintenance procedures at the 'Brush be far different from those at the Pulpit.

This course, says Hurdzan, "follows the natural flow of the terrain, utilizing fescue fairways which are kept hard and dry, allowing golfers quite a bit of bump-and-run play, as do the courses of the British Isles. The greens are bentgrass and generally very large, counterbalancing the abundance of sand bunkers of the course. Devil's Paintbrush is a course that golf purists will love." And not just golf traditionalists love it: The Paintbrush has received a number of accolades from environmental groups as an example of how environmentally friendly a world-famous golf course can be.

While no one affiliated with the

course will admit to a signature hole, the par-5 17th remains tattooed on one's memory. "When Chris [Haney] first showed me the site, he said, 'There are a couple of things I want you to save.' Two of those things were an abandoned barn foundation and the farm house foundation," says Hurdzan. "Both were made of stacked stone and although they were at least 100 years old, they were in remarkably good condition. We set the tees so the landing area is right at the ruins. So I made the fairway about 102 yards wide, with the ruins having the effect of dividing it into three distinct landing areas."

What a hole. The right landing area is about 30 yards wide, with out of bounds to its right. The left is about 40 yards wide, twice the size of the centre target zone. Landing in the ruins will cost you a one-stroke penalty, while the second shot from the left must carry a 120-foot-long, 12-foot-high sod-wall bunker. The tiny green is perched, making it a difficult target.

Their clubhouses symbolize the vast difference between the Pulpit and the

The principals of the Devil's Pulpit Golf Association journeyed to Britain before any work commenced on their new venture, Devil's Paintbrush. Accompanying them was course architect Michael Hurdzan, who had previously designed Devil's Pulpit. While the Pulpit was the epitome of 1990s extravagance, the Paintbrush was to be "just like Scotland" in one founder's words. As you can see, the trip across the Atlantic paid dividends for golfers in Ontario. (Although this poor chap might disagree!)

From the second tee of the Devil's Paintbrush, you can see the CN Tower on Toronto's waterfront some 70 kilometres distant. But why would you want to take your eyes off the golf course?

Paintbrush. The swanky 18,000-square-foot Pulpit mansion offers gourmet cuisine year-round, cocktails at the longest bar of any golf club in Canada, swimming pool, whirlpool, sauna, billiards room, fully stocked pro shop, expansive practice area, and a shuttle service from the cart storage building. (That cart building is so attractive that first-time guests often mistake it for the clubhouse.)

In contrast, the Paintbrush's 3,000-square-foot Tudor-style clubhouse is little more than "a glorified halfway house," says its architect. There isn't even a locker room. But, in true Haney and Abbott style, every detail has been observed. Under its vaulted 30-foot-high ceilings, golfers enjoy a pub-style atmosphere, complete with a wide selection of draught beers and a delicious, though limited menu. Like the course it presides over, this building definitely owes its heritage to golf as it is played over 'ome.

Perhaps Glen Abbey's most spec-
tacular sight: from the 11th tee,
players hit into a river valley
some 120 feet below.

GLEN ABBEY

Golf Club

Architect: Jack Nicklaus
Head Professional: Bob Lean
Manager: Jack McClellan
Superintendent: Dean Baker

"The shrine of Canadian golf." Perhaps that is putting it a bit strongly, but there is no doubt that Glen Abbey Golf Club is more, much more, than just another public golf course.

The "shrine" phrase first appears in press reports about plans put forth in the early 1970s by the Royal Canadian Golf Association and Great Northern Capital Inc. to develop a permanent site for the Canadian Open, the world's fourth-oldest national championship, hosted by the RCGA. The association's headquarters would be on the site, housing the offices of the people who govern organized amateur golf in this country as well as the Canadian Golf Hall of Fame and Museum.

The religious analogy might have been encouraged not only by the fact that the existing building on the site north of Oakville, Ontario, had been used as a Jesuit retreat, but also by the "golfing god" contracted to design the course: the legendary Jack Nicklaus.

Richard Grimm, now the RCGA's director of professional tournaments, was the organization's president back in 1972 and had acted as chairman of the Open which was held that year at Cherry Hill near Fort Erie, Ontario. When approached by Rod McIsaac of Great Northern, Grimm was leery. "He told me he liked watching the tournament, but it was his feeling that the gallery was not given a fair shake for viewing," Grimm recalled later. "Immediately I thought, 'Here's another gripe from a spectator.' But then he threw me a country mile by saying he had a piece of property in Oakville — and we were thinking about a permanent site. The result of that conversation was meetings with the RCGA, Jack Nicklaus, the Abbey Glen Property Corporation and Imperial Tobacco Limited (longtime sponsors of the Open), and the result of those meetings was Glen Abbey." That "result" has played host to every Canadian Open since 1977, with the exception of 1980 when the national championship was played at Royal Montreal.

When McIsaac made his proposal, more than 200 acres remained of the 350 that mining magnate Andre Dorfman purchased in 1929 to build an imposing castle-like home for himself and his new wife. Sold in 1953 to the Jesuits, it became available later when Rome ruled that the priests could better serve the church in Toronto. Some of the land was already used for golf, but the layout was unsuitable for the national championship.

Nicklaus, whose professional career was at its peak, had decided to lend his talent to golf course architecture. What he was faced with at Glen Abbey, the first design project he had undertaken on his own, was a schizophrenic situation: most of the land was flat and relatively undistinguished, but the remainder was wonderful river valley land snaking along the meandering Sixteen Mile Creek in the shadow of spectacular bluffs.

More than one million cubic feet of earth were moved to massage the flat land into a fine test of golf, "a panorama of gently rolling fairways," in Nicklaus's words. In excess of 100,000 cubic yards of topsoil became mounds, designed to give spectators at Glen Abbey the

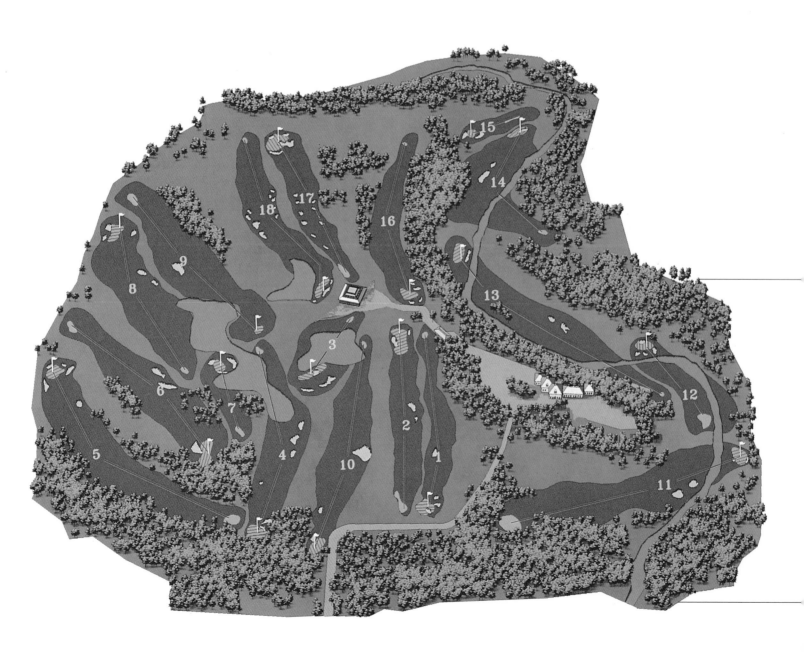

The par-four 14th is considered one of the tougher holes on the PGA Tour.

Glen Abbey Golf Club Oakville, Ontario				Hole	Yards	Par
	Length	Par	Rating	1	443	4
				2	414	4
Gold	7102	73	75.5	3	156	3
Blue	6618	73	72.5	4	417	4
White	6202	73	70.5	5	527	5
Yellow	5577	74	73.5	6	437	4
				7	197	3
				8	433	4
				9	458	4
				OUT	3482	35
				10	435	5
				11	452	4
				12	187	3
				13	529	5
				14	426	4
				15	141	3
				16	516	5
				17	434	4
				18	500	5
				IN	3620	38
				Total	7102	73

"fair shake" McIsaac pined for by acting as natural amphitheatres. "It is the best spectator course in the world," the designer said upon its completion in 1976. But it is the five holes along the creek, the "valley holes" kickstarted by a drive off the 11th tee into a gorge some 120 feet below, that burn themselves into the memories of competitors and spectators alike. These holes have the reputation of being one of the toughest stretches on the entire PGA Tour.

The 11th fairway, squeezed by trees on the left and bunkers on the right, ends abruptly. For at that point, Sixteen Mile Creek, ill-named because it is closer to a river in nature and has been known to tear out bridges when swollen by rain, flows across the hole. On the other side of the creek, the undulating green awaits, well bunkered and tucked in at the base of those towering bluffs. The waterway comes into play again on the par-three 12th, twice on the 13th (passing in front of the tee, continuing down the left boundary and then slicing back in front of the green, daring you to go for the long, narrow green in two shots) and on the par-four 14th, where it has claimed many a sliced drive. This has traditionally been one of the toughest holes on the course for the PGA Tour pros, with the stroke average approaching 4.5 some years. That average is inflated not only by the presence of the creek, but also by the swale that cuts through the centre of the rolling green, making three-putts commonplace.

While Glen Abbey can stretch up to 7,100 yards for the Canadian Open, the only PGA Tour event held outside the United States, a variety of tee positions offer distances right down to 5,200. "I regard the emphasis on length and huge greens as the two worst faults of modern golf course design," said Nicklaus. "Many people assume my golf courses will be long monsters, but I consider golf to be a game of precision, not strength." To his credit, Nicklaus kept in mind that the PGA Tour is at Glen Abbey for but one week each year. The rest of the 30,000 rounds are played by public golfers.

Nicklaus and Glen Abbey are linked in one more way, apparently for all time: Of all his Tour victories, 70 in total, none is a Canadian Open. He has been the runner-up an unbelievable seven times.

The slick greens at Glen Abbey, like the 12th, are among the best in the country.

From the fourteenth green, Glen Abbey ascends from the spectacular river valley.

How The Pros Play Glen Abbey

For Dave Barr, the veteran PGA Tour pro from British Columbia, one key to success at Glen Abbey is the left-to-right shot. Barr, who has finished as high as fourth in the Canadian Open here, believes the two toughest holes on the course are eight and nine. On the eighth, he tries to play down the left side beside the two bunkers, which leaves an open shot to the green with a long-iron. The key to the ninth, a long par-four, is keeping the ball in the fairway. "If you end up in the (right-side) bunker, you have to play a 210-yard sand shot," he said prior to the 1990 Open. Ironically, it was in that very situation that he found himself during the final round of the tournament. Taking only a minute amount of sand on the downswing with his two-iron meant a "fat" shot that found the pond some 50 yards short of the green. The resulting triple-bogey took him out of contention.

When he plays the Abbey, Barr believes he will score well if he can get through holes eight to 11 in even-par. The 13th hole, a 529-yard par-five, can be reached with two mighty blows. "I usually won't go for it unless I'm 220 yards or less from the green," says Barr, who has won more than $1 million on the pro tours.

On both 14, the 426-yard par-four, and 15, a par-three of 141 yards, the severe slope of the green means keeping the ball below the hole is a necessity. "The key to 16 is staying in the fairway," says Barr of the 516-yard par-five. "You can usually reach it in two from either side of the fairway. There's a good chance for a birdie here."

The 17th hole again favors a fade to stay away from the deep bunkers on the left. A good tee shot is rewarded with a short-iron approach. The 18th, a 500-yard par-five, has been called one of the great finishing holes. It tempts players to go for the green in two, but taunts them with a large pond in front of the long, narrow green. Three of the last six holes at the Abbey are par-fives, a situation that has made for some exciting conclusions to past Canadian Opens.

The East Course at Hamilton Golf and Country Club is the newest of the three nines, but is comparable to the original 18 in design and challenge.

———— Ancaster, Ontario ————

HAMILTON

Golf and Country Club

*Architect: Harry Colt (18)
and C.E. Robinson (9)
Head Professional: Rob McDannold
Manager: John Mickle
Superintendent: Rod Trainor*

Driving up to the stately, ivy-enveloped mansion which serves as the clubhouse for the Hamilton Golf and Country Club, even the most jaded golfer realizes that here is something extraordinary. The quiet, superlative elegance of both the course and the club is seldom matched anywhere in the world of golf.

The Hamilton Golf and Country Club was once located in the city of Hamilton, on the present site of the Hamilton Centre Mall, when it was founded in 1894. A couple of years later, yielding to the pressures of urban growth and accompanying tax pressures as many city courses did in those days, the club moved to acreage on the side of Hamilton Mountain. This location, now the Chedoke municipal course, served the membership until 1913 when the club's fathers decided to build 18 holes and an imposing clubhouse farther up the face of Hamilton Mountain, where the topography and view were unequalled.

Harry Colt, riding the success of his acclaimed new course at England's Sunningdale and the Toronto Golf Club, was contracted to design the layout. Drawing on his British heritage, he crafted a fine bump-and-run course which officially opened in 1916. At Sunningdale, Colt gave a hint of what would eventually be

one of his great contributions to golf course architecture: comprehensive tree-planting programs.

The site of Hamilton Golf and Country Club, which now covers more than 300 acres, was largely farmer's fields when the course was designed, a situation unimaginable to a present-day visitor. In the mind of present Head Professional Rob McDannold, Colt's visionary genius is unsurpassed: "When you look at the original map of this property, there were almost no trees. Now it looks as if it was carved out of the forest. Colt planned it so there are exact gaps in the trees for sunlight, for the wind, for shots. He had an absolutely amazing ability to foresee what this course would look like 50 years later. The trees look like they've been here forever."

An immediate success upon its opening, the Hamilton Golf and Country Club played host to the Canadian Open just three years later. The first national championship played after the end of the First World War, it drew more than usual interest for a number of reasons, not the least of which was the fact that it

Surrounded by forest and dotted with ponds and streams, Hamilton is a shotmaker's delight.

counted the great U.S. amateur Bobby Jones among the field. But Jones could do no better than a tie with Ottawa's Karl Keffer for second, as Douglas Edgar of Atlanta, Georgia, won the first of his two consecutive Open titles. Edgar's four-round total of 278 was at that time the world record for professionals. The second, and final, time the club opened its course to the Open, in 1930, Tommy Armour of Detroit defeated fellow PGA Tour pro Leo Diegel in a 36-hole playoff. To get into the playoff, Armour had to craft a stunning 64 in the final round, a course record at the time. Jim Nelford of Vancouver tied it in the 1977 Canadian Amateur, but still finished second to Rod Spittle. It has been recently broken by Warren Sye, who shot a stunning 62.

Playing the original 18 holes (the West and South nines) today can be very reminiscent of those early days when Jones and Armour trod Hamilton's fairways, for an astute membership has taken care to maintain the original design in large part. The rolling fairways are separated by those now-mature trees and the design is as valuable and serviceable as a fine

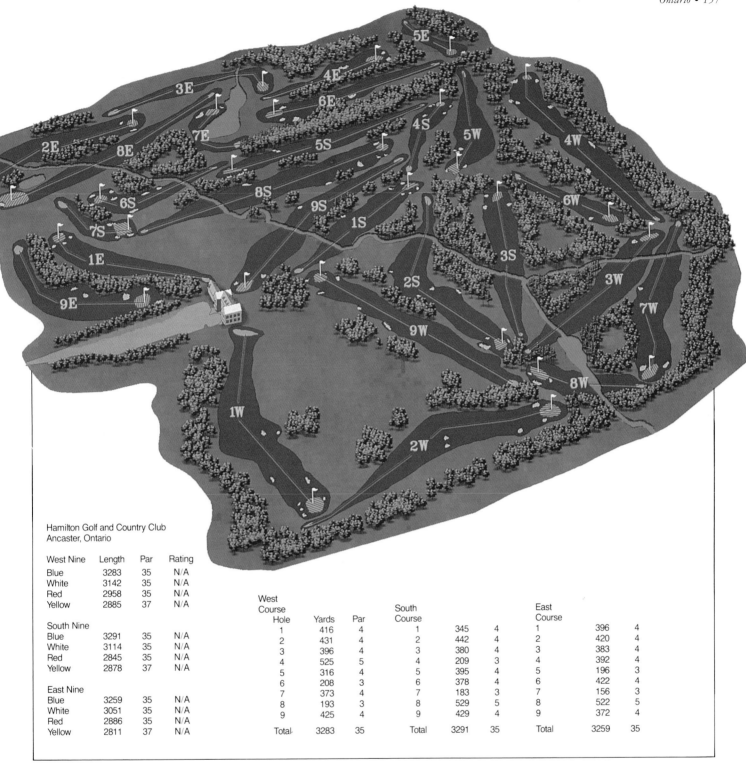

Hamilton Golf and Country Club
Ancaster, Ontario

West Nine	Length	Par	Rating
Blue	3283	35	N/A
White	3142	35	N/A
Red	2958	35	N/A
Yellow	2885	37	N/A
South Nine			
Blue	3291	35	N/A
White	3114	35	N/A
Red	2845	35	N/A
Yellow	2878	37	N/A
East Nine			
Blue	3259	35	N/A
White	3051	35	N/A
Red	2886	35	N/A
Yellow	2811	37	N/A

West Course Hole	Yards	Par	South Course			East Course		
1	416	4	1	345	4	1	396	4
2	431	4	2	442	4	2	420	4
3	396	4	3	380	4	3	383	4
4	525	5	4	209	3	4	392	4
5	316	4	5	395	4	5	196	3
6	208	3	6	378	4	6	422	4
7	373	4	7	183	3	7	156	3
8	193	3	8	529	5	8	522	5
9	425	4	9	429	4	9	372	4
Total	3283	35	Total	3291	35	Total	3259	35

antique. Colt, the first golf course architect who was not a professional golfer, nonetheless has managed to provide a fine test of golf. With only two par-fives, this beautifully conditioned 6,600-yard layout plays much longer than the card indicates.

While the course is not overly tight, well-positioned tee shots are vital to a respectable score. The majority of the par-fours require good planning and execution to prepare for the most advantageous approach to the green. Straying into the stands of mature hardwoods seldom means a lost ball, but those massive trees will no doubt prevent advancing it once found. The par-threes at Hamilton are strong: all but one play to more than 180 yards from the blue tees and more than 175 from the whites.

"The first four holes can make or break you," says McDannold. "It's a very difficult start. The first two holes are par-fours of more than 400 yards. Your first drive has to be about 240 yards into the prevailing wind to the corner of the dogleg. You can't cut the corner, unless you can hit it at least 270, because the corner is filled with hills, valleys, pot bunkers and so on. So you have to play right, even though that gives you a longer shot in to a well-bunkered green. Number 2 is a dogleg-right, with bunkers right and trees left, that requires a long, accurate drive. The green has lots of bunkers and you're dealing with that wind again as you hit anything from a two- to a five-iron in.

"The third hole demands another accurate drive, but no more than 235 yards, otherwise you'll be down a steep slope covered with rough. Hit a long-iron off the tee, and you'll have about 165 in to an elevated green with a shelf. Don't be long on this one. The fourth hole can give you a bit of a reprieve if you hit it straight off the tee. In a tournament, I wouldn't hit driver off the tee here. There's a pit left, so stay a little right, but notice the trees and fairway bunkers down that side. This hole is reachable, but there's so many opportunities

to get into trouble that I would just accept it being a three-shot hole and try to get close with that third shot. The green is long, narrow and elevated, bunkered left and front."

In 1975, the growing membership was placing an enormous burden on Colt's 18 holes, so the decision was made to bring in noted Canadian architect C.E. (Robbie) Robinson to design an additional nine holes of a complementary nature. "The East nine is spectacular," enthuses McDannold. "It's very tight; a great members' course."

It should be noted that Nicol Thompson, elder brother of talented course architect Stanley Thompson, served as the head professional at the Hamilton Golf and Country Club for 50 years until his retirement in 1945. He was succeeded by Dick Borthwick (1946-74), Ken Steeves (1975-80), Gary Maue (1981-89) and McDannold.

The third hole on the West Course requires an iron off the tee and a mid-iron to hold the elevated green.

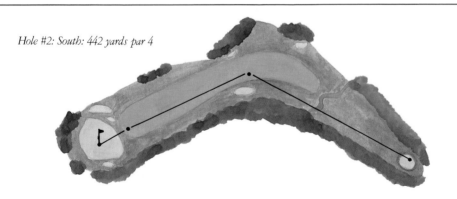

Hole #2: South: 442 yards par 4

The greens at Hamilton are not overly large, but are subtle and fast.

The Toughest Hole at Hamilton

"The second hole on our South course is the toughest of our 27," says Hamilton Head Professional Rob McDannold, "and I think it's one of the very best in Canada." Playing 442 yards from the blue tees and 406 from the whites, this hole demands a 230-yard drive to the corner of the dogleg-left. The mature stand of trees in the corner deters long-ball hitters from trying to carry the dogleg. McDannold suggests a three-wood off the tee, since a driver might carry the ball through the fairway. "From there, it's all uphill into the wind to an elevated green with a steep bunker right and trees, a slope and rough left," says the pro. "I tell most people to play up short of the green on their second shot and play it as a par-five; it saves them a lot of grief."

The Heron Point experience combines three distinct styles: Carolina lowlands, linksland, and traditional parkland.

HERON POINT

Golf Links

Private

So tell us, Tom McBroom, what is the most interesting thing about your renowned creation, Heron Point Golf Links? "It was a trailer park when I first saw the property. I was shocked. There were about 300 ugly house trailers clustered randomly around the lake. It was like hillbilly heaven."

But McBroom, a highly respected course architect based in Toronto, saw far beyond those trailers. In his mind's eye was a great golf course, sprawling over the 250 acres of rolling hills, marshes and forest just outside of Hamilton, Ontario. The one thing that really caught his attention was the large lake in the middle of the property. Instead of being ringed by house trailers, it now drives the irrigation system and forms the backbone of the course, especially the heroic ninth and 18th holes.

The multi-faceted nature of the acreage allowed McBroom to introduce three distinct themes into the design. Although

Architect Tom McBroom brought home some mementos from his visits to British courses. Note the pot bunkers on the par-5 sixth hole.

the course is called Heron Point Golf Links, he says the links style represents just one of its characteristics.

"There are some linksy holes, that are not treed, where we've lined the fairways with fescue grass to give that British feel. The style of the bunkering is definitely British: small pottish bunkers dug well into the ground, not flashy. I've been in Britain several times and that's helped me discover some themeing elements that I've tried to reproduce in my courses, like at Heron Point.

"There are the marshland, or low-country, holes that you might see in the Carolinas or Florida, where you have to hit shots over the marshland to targets. That would be holes eight and thirteen and, to a lesser extent, five and six. On the par 3s — eight and thirteen — you hit from bank to bank over a marsh and then travel to the green over a boardwalk," McBroom says, adding that this style is very environmentally acceptable.

"With this type of hole, you're really not constructing a fairway or filling the wetland, which is unacceptable. The negative is that it creates a definite target-style hole and that is, by definition, usually an all-or-nothing hole. The challenge is to set the tees so it is as playable as possible for everyone.

"And then we've got wooded holes like 15, 16, 17, and 18. They are really parkland-style holes. There's not a lot of artificial contouring there; most of it was natural."

Far from creating a schizophrenic golf experience, McBroom's bold concept succeeds admirably in providing a well-integrated and unique layout. Each golf hole stands on its own merits, yet melds together at the end of the day into a memorable outing.

Like some other McBroom courses, Heron Point punishes those foolhardy enough to play from the wrong tees. Played at the appropriate yardage, its perceived difficulty softens, offering the occasional birdie opportunity. No matter what

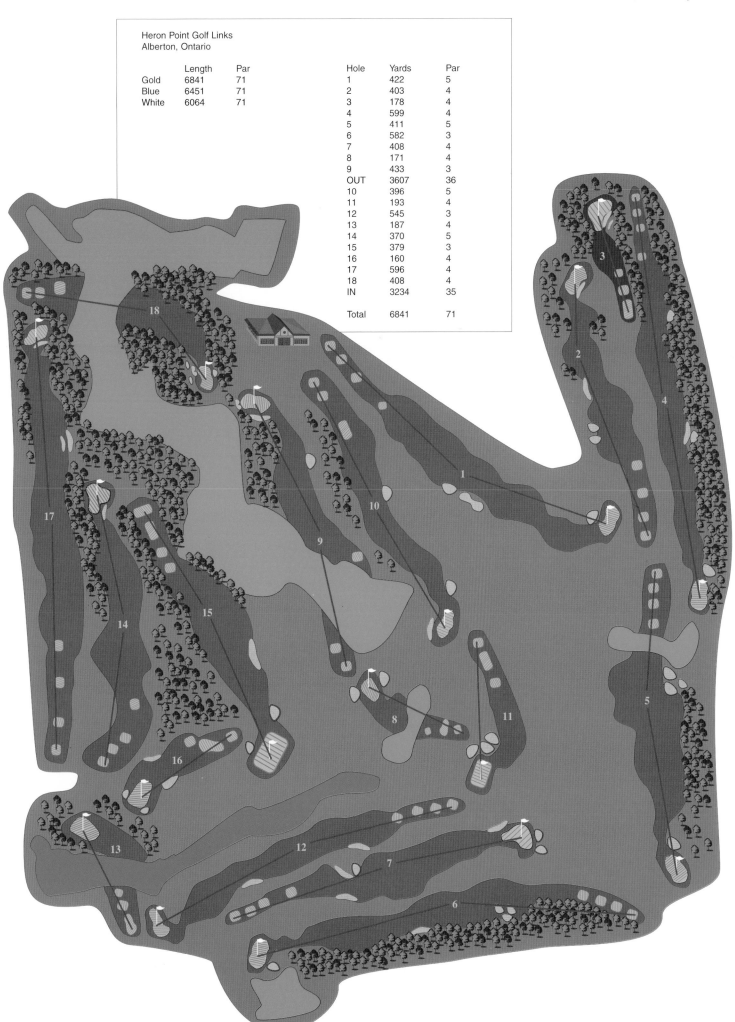

Heron Point Golf Links
Alberton, Ontario

	Length	Par
Gold	6841	71
Blue	6451	71
White	6064	71

Hole	Yards	Par
1	422	5
2	403	4
3	178	4
4	599	4
5	411	5
6	582	3
7	408	4
8	171	4
9	433	3
OUT	3607	36
10	396	5
11	193	4
12	545	3
13	187	4
14	370	5
15	379	3
16	160	4
17	596	4
18	408	4
IN	3234	35
Total	6841	71

The final hole at Heron Point: A gut-wrenching drive from the back tee deck will carry the water – maybe.

tees are used, however, the ever-present marshes, fescue, and forest combine to ensure errant shots do not go unpunished.

"You have to hit the ball where you are supposed to," says McBroom. "The more you play the course, the more you under-stand each hole's strategy. You learn to lay back on the par 5s unless you've really tagged the drive, and at least two of the par 5s are designed to be unreachable under most circumstances. I think one of the signs of a good course is when it tells the player when to attack and when to lay back."

But McBroom also admits that, unless the wind is up, Heron Point can be mas-tered. It's played host to the Canadian Masters, one of the key Canadian Tour events, since 1994. For example, in 1997, Steven Alker of New Zealand fired a stun-ning 10-under 62 in the final round to pull him into a four-way tie for second, eight shots behind winner Mike Weir of Bright's Grove, Ontario.

The architect feels no shame when low scores are posted on his courses. In fact, he provides a counter-argument for those who insist that courses are being made obsolete by modern technology.

"These players are so good. There's just a hair's breadth between them and the PGA Tour. [In fact, Weir qualified for the U.S. PGA Tour later in 1997.] It doesn't matter what you do. They all drive it long and down the middle. They get into that rhythm and everything is six to ten feet from the pin. Combine that with a hot putter, and bingo! You've got your 62.

"There's really nothing the architect can do without going to extremes. Why destroy a good piece of land just to pre-vent a tour pro from going 10-under? I'm not affronted if a tour pro shoots a 62 on one of my courses. I'm delighted for him. And I'm delighted that the average golfer can go out the next day and have a good round, too."

Tom McBroom, Heron Point's architect, loves to talk about the ninth and eighteenth holes at this course. "They are two very unique finishing holes. I think they could be called 'heroic' holes, although you don't hear that term very often any more. But these two redefine heroic. You've got to hit the big blow over the water or you're dead. Each of those drives is a little different, however. On nine, it could be called a 'strategic heroic' drive because you have to not only get it over the water, but you have to angle the shot right to left. You have to turn the shot over because the hole doglegs right to left. The carry isn't that long and it's a huge, wide landing area, but the difference on your second shot can be between a 2-iron and a 7-iron. A good player will sense

the strategy of the hole and execute the shot, and then he's in good shape.

"The 18th hole is a super finishing hole, a hole which could easily decide a match. The carry over the lake from the back tee is 235 yards and you've got to hit the drive dead solid and straight. Then you have to hit another perfect shot to a narrow elevated and bunkered green."

Parts of the Heron Point property offer vistas of adjoining holes, much like traditional links layouts.

A reachable par-5, the fifth hole calls for a precise approach to the green.

KING VALLEY

Golf Club

Architect: Doug Carrick
Head Professional: Greg Shephard
Manager: Stan Waterhouse

King Valley is aptly named. Everything associated with it is regal, ranging from the awe-inspiring Tudor mansion which serves as an elegantly appointed clubhouse, to the equally impressive golf course which, although built in the early 1990s, has the look and feel of a mature classic.

Toronto's Doug Carrick, a very talented course architect with a instinctive feel for traditional design, was presented with an incredibly beautiful valley north of Toronto that cried out for a golf course: 165 acres of towering pines, majestic maples, beech and oaks, with tiny ponds dotting the undulating topography. The result harks back to the wonderful era of Canadian Stanley Thompson, Donald Ross and their colleagues 70 years ago,

It didn't take long for the King Valley course to gain a reputation for offering a memorable golf experience in a region of the country that is blessed with some of the best courses in the world. And when the owners, King Valley Development Corporation, constructed the stunningly opulent clubhouse, the legend of King Valley was complete.

Walking up the flagstone path leading to the clubhouse, it is almost impossible to believe that you are not approaching a historic English country manor. Its setting is breathtaking, framed

The 12th hole is a spectacular and challenging par 3.

King Valley Golf Club
King City, Ontario

	Length	Par	Rating
Gold	6905	72	NA
Blue	6597	72	NA
White	6204	72	NA
Red	5552	73	NA

Hole	Yards	Par			
1	408	4	10	372	4
2	169	3	11	350	4
3	409	4	12	217	3
4	412	4	13	429	4
5	501	5	14	505	5
6	403	4	15	437	4
7	199	3	16	166	3
8	491	5	17	419	4
9	433	4	18	585	5
OUT	3425	36	IN	3480	3
			Total	6905	72

by wildflowers and stands of trees. The edifice (the mere word "building" does not convey its splendor) — complete with brick and limestone facade and wood shingles trimmed with copper flashing — is sculpted into the side of a ravine, offering commanding views of the ninth, 12th and 18th holes.

Every conceivable amenity is available to members of King Valley and their guests. Among those offered are valet parking and bag transportation, limousine service, a private study with complete secretarial services, specialty wine cellar and a billiards room.

No wonder that King Valley says that while "it is reserved for the select few, it will be the envy of many."

Obviously, no expense has been spared to make King Valley stand head and shoulders above its not inconsiderable competition. That is reinforced by the presence of Curtis Strange,

two-time winner of both the Canadian and U.S. Opens, on the club's marketing materials. Strange was retained by the owners as a design consultant and course advisor. "King Valley is a natural," says Strange. "It's a classic golfer's golf course set in a spectacular environment."

King Valley chose to offer transferable memberships, meaning that members who leave the club for whatever reason may sell, lease or otherwise transfer their memberships. The obvious advantage this plan has over traditional memberships is that the member doesn't lose his initiation fee should he have to leave the club.

While King Valley has retained the traditional values of the "Golden Age of Golf," Carrick has utilized all the modern-day innovations to provide the consummate golfing experience for those fortunate enough to play here. Aside from double-row irrigation,

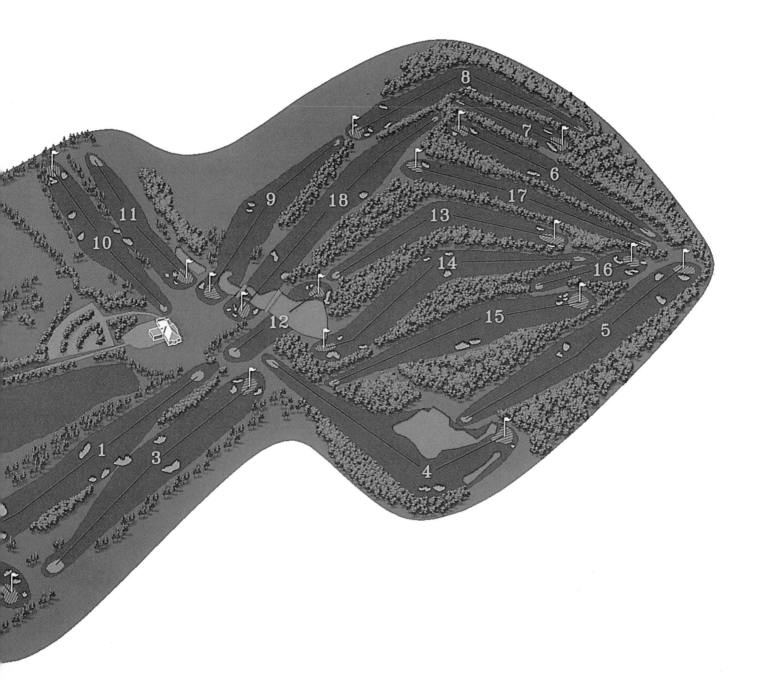

The Most Dangerous Hole at King Valley

Termed the "most dangerous hole" in King Valley's excellent course narrative, the 412-yard fourth is a spectacular par 4 played from an elevated tee.It is a dogleg left which curls around a large pond which extends all the wayto the green. A long, straight  tee shot placed as close to the pond as you dare leaves a short iron to a narrow green. A pond lurks on the right side of the green, creating an island effect. A narrow neck of fairway leads into the green for the more cautious player who may wish to run the ball up, since an approach which goes long will end up in a bunker in the back right corner.

Number 14 is an outstanding double-dogleg par 5.

King Valley's 18th is a fine finishing hole with a pond in front of the green.

Ohio bunker sand and splendid bentgrass playing surfaces, there is a six-acre multi-featured practice facility complete with bentgrass tees, target greens, putting and chipping greens with a variety of grassy hollows and mounds as well as two practice bunkers.

The design of the course itself is superbly well-balanced, with a par of 36 on each nine, consisting of four par 3s, 10 par 4s and four par 5s of varying lengths. Expect to use every club in your bag and to be tested for length, accuracy and finesse.

Aside from the par-4 fourth (see sidebar), King Valley's hole-by-hole narrative identifies Numbers 8, 9 and 18 as "signature holes".

The eighth hole, a 491-yard par 5 from the back tees, is a dogleg left through a spruce and pine plantation on the first portion of the fairway and then through a hardwood bush on the second. The ideal tee shot must carry 250 yards over a bunker in the corner of the dogleg. The second shot is then played across a small valley and stream, rising back up the hill to an elevated, tilted green guarded by three steep-faced bunkers and out of bounds on the right.

The subsequent hole is an exhilarating downhill par 4, with the tee situated at the highest point of the course and offering tremendous views of the surrounding countryside. A long tee shot down the right side leaves the best approach onto the green with a middle iron. The undulating green is protected on the right by a menacing bunker and a pond on the left front. Avoid being above the hole.

Your round at King Valley concludes with a spectacular par 5 sprawling 585 yards down a slope to a green severed from the fairway by a pond. The tee shot is played from a slightly elevated tee to the fairway which is canted from right to left. One bunker on the left and grassy hollows on the right cut into the hillside to protect the first landing area. The second shot must be placed beyond a bunker flanking the right side of the second landing area, setting up a short iron approach across the pond onto the angled green. A bunker on the front left of the green combine with three more to the right and rear to add to the unique challenge of King Valley's final hole.

Walking off the 18th green, gazing up at the imposing yet hospitable clubhouse, you will concur with Curtis Strange, who says: "I have gone around my share of golf courses in my career as a golf professional. The King Valley course is very special — a natural, and destined to become a classic."

At 479 yards from the back tees, the par-4 ninth hole typifies the Lake Joseph Club experience. Set in Ontario's Muskoka tourist region, it features rocky outcrops, water, bush, and stunning scenery.

LAKE JOSEPH

Club

Private

Secluded among the lakes, granite faces, and primeval forests in Ontario's spectacular Muskoka tourist region is the Lake Joseph Club, one of the superb stable of courses owned by ClubLink Corporation, Canada's largest owner and operator of golf facilities. And, like many of ClubLink's other properties, Lake Joseph was designed by renowned Canadian architect Thomas McBroom.

"The Lake Joseph Club is characterized by magnificent trees, bold rock outcrops, and the sensual and striking landscape of Muskoka," says McBroom. "My task here was not so much to create a theme, but to let the beauty of the land itself speak out. The lines and contours of the golf course therefore are relatively gentle and soft, and artificial contouring and highlighting are unnecessary."

McBroom accomplished that and more. Both *Golf Digest* and *SCORE* magazine selected Lake Joseph as the best new

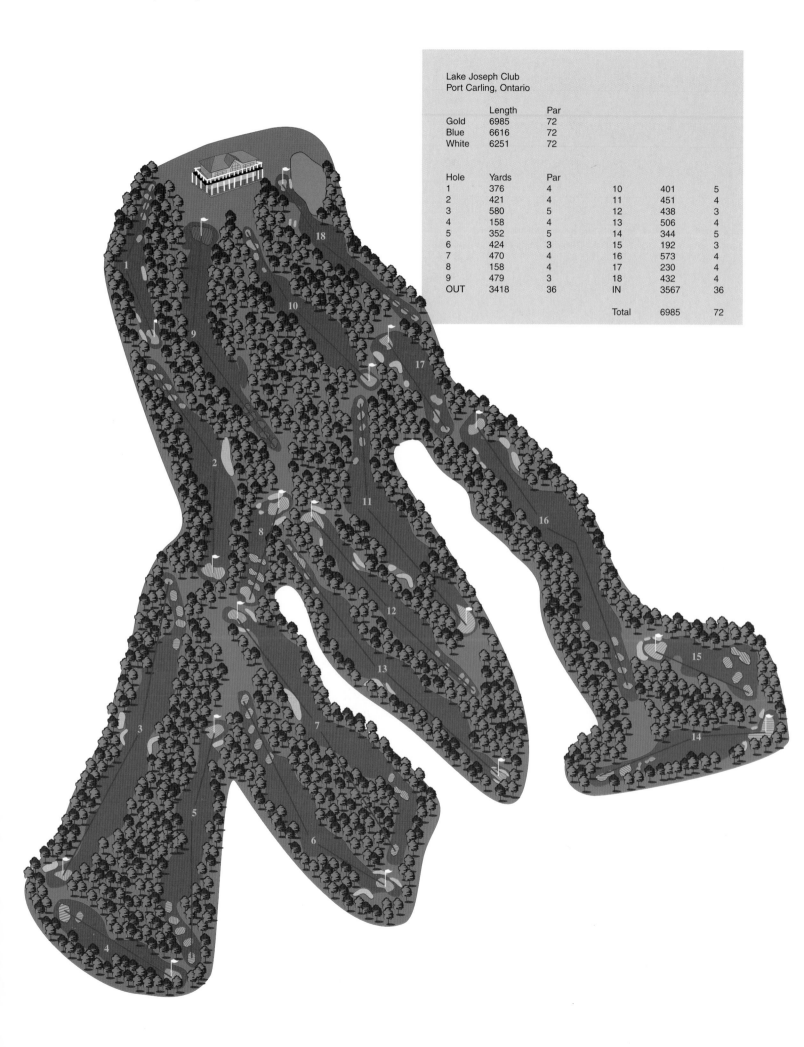

Lake Joseph Club
Port Carling, Ontario

	Length	Par
Gold	6985	72
Blue	6616	72
White	6251	72

Hole	Yards	Par			
1	376	4	10	401	5
2	421	4	11	451	4
3	580	5	12	438	3
4	158	4	13	506	4
5	352	5	14	344	5
6	424	3	15	192	3
7	470	4	16	573	4
8	158	4	17	230	4
9	479	3	18	432	4
OUT	3418	36	IN	3567	36
			Total	6985	72

A few holes at Lake Joseph, like the 438-yard 12th, have a linksy feel to them, in contrast to several others which are entwined in the Canadian Shield.

course in the country in 1997. Integral to those honours was the recognition by the selectors that the architect had integrated the very elements that make a course in this rugged region of Canada unique.

"In laying out the fairways and green sites, I tried very hard to seek out natural bowls, valleys and draws upon which the fairways and greens could be developed without undue grading or manipulation of the land," McBroom says. "I wanted there to be a feeling of naturalness and receptivity such that individual holes fit upon the landscape, rather than lying forcefully imposed upon it. I wanted the golf holes to appear as if they had always been there, while showing off the spectacular beauty of Muskoka. The granite cliff which forms the backdrop of the par-3 eighth hole, the magnificent view from the 16th tee, or the utilization of the wetland on No. 11 as a natural hazard are just a few examples of where the land and the golf course are in perfect harmony."

The same principle of restraint applies to the style of the bunkers and greens. In contrast to some of McBroom's earlier works, the greens are simple in form and contour and free from complex undulation. The gentle putting surfaces contrast with the complexity of the surrounding landscape, providing balance and relief. Difficulty on the greens was not a design prerequisite, since the challenges at Lake Joseph fall elsewhere. The true difficulty here is not so much focussed on one particular facet of the course, but is rather a sum of all the parts. Any time there are 18 holes carved through dense mixed forest and routed over severe and rocky terrain, there is an inherent difficulty. McBroom was mature and wise enough to realize he did not have to contrive any artificial challenges; nature had beaten him to it.

The same principles apply to the design of the bunkers which, in many cases, play a far more important role than

The diabolical par-4 finishing hole at Lake Joseph requires an accurate tee shot and a precise approach to a large green in order to avoid the usual bogey.

mere penal hazards or visual enhancement. In fact, the bunkers at Lake Joseph can often work for the golfer rather than against him. They provide artistic accent where appropriate and as a line of play by acting as distinct targets. They highlight attractive features such as the magnificent white pine adjacent to the 18th green or the rock outcropping near the landing area on No. 9. Bunkers are intended only as hazards where a degree of difficulty is important to the course strategy. In general, the form of the bunkers, like the putting surfaces, is simple and free from artificiality.

Although the Lake Joseph course can be visually intimidating, McBroom says he went to extreme lengths to ensure "a high level of challenge, fairness, and pleasure for golfers of all skill levels." Otherwise known as "playability," McBroom says it is much tougher to create a truly playable course than it is to build a severely difficult brute of a layout. "To achieve playability, four different sets of tees have been designed with tremendous length and approach angle variation

between them. The principle is to equalize golfers of vastly different skill levels by placing them on the appropriate tee from which they can hit the specific target, given a reasonable drive."

Not content with a superb 18 holes, ClubLink commissioned McBroom to design a nine-hole short course on the site of the teaching academy adjacent to the main course. "The short course is one of the important amenities of a true destination resort and caters to families — beginners, seniors, children, or parents who want to play with their children," McBroom says. "The beauty of the short course is that it is variable in length, allowing everything from a 2-iron to a wedge. With the same overall yardage as the short course at Augusta National, players can hit every iron in the bag, while enjoying a leisurely round."

While you must be a member to play Lake Joseph, the upside is that your membership allows you to play any of ClubLink's other excellent courses as well.

Lake Joseph Club: Standing on the first tee at the splendid Lake Joseph Club in Ontario's Muskoka tourist region makes you long to be a member of ClubLink. This company, the largest owner, operator, and developer of golf facilities in Canada, has acquired some of the country's finest properties in a few short years. Among these courses, all in Ontario, are Heron Point Golf Links, Greystone and RattleSnake Point in Milton, and King Valley Golf Club in Aurora, where ClubLink's corporate offices are located. As this book was going to the printer, ClubLink had made an offer to purchase Glen Abbey Golf Club in Oakville, Ontario, home of the Canadian Open, the Royal Canadian Golf Association, and the Canadian Ladies' Golf Association.

Lake Joseph's par 3s add tremendously to an already memorable experience. This is the 158-yard eighth hole.

Extensive water, mounding and bunkering, indicate your strategy at Lionhead.

—————— *Brampton, Ontario* ——————

LIONHEAD

Golf and Country Club

Architect: Ted Baker
Head Professional: Chuck Lorimer
General Manager: Alan Ogilvie
Superintendent: Jim Molenhuis

Lionhead roared into existence in 1991, calling itself "the most 'private' public golf facility in Canada," and it has never looked back. Its stated goal was to provide a golfing experience for the public that previously had been available only at the best private clubs. Many knowledgeable observers feel it attained that goal almost from the day the doors opened.

"Lionhead has the fastest greens outside of the Masters tournament itself," said PGA Tour pro Dave Barr after winning the nationally televised 1991 Cadillac Classic skins game at Lionhead. "The Legends nine could very well become the most famous nine holes of golf in the world," echoed 1991 British Open winner Ian Baker-Finch after an outing at the then 27-hole facility. (Lionhead expanded to 36 holes early in the 1993 season.)

Like these players, golf writers tend to rave over the stunning layout that crisscrosses a river valley just outside Brampton. "Lionhead is a gem to watch for in the world's top 100," predicted the Toronto Star. Golf Digest said it was "one of the best courses, public or private, to be found anywhere."

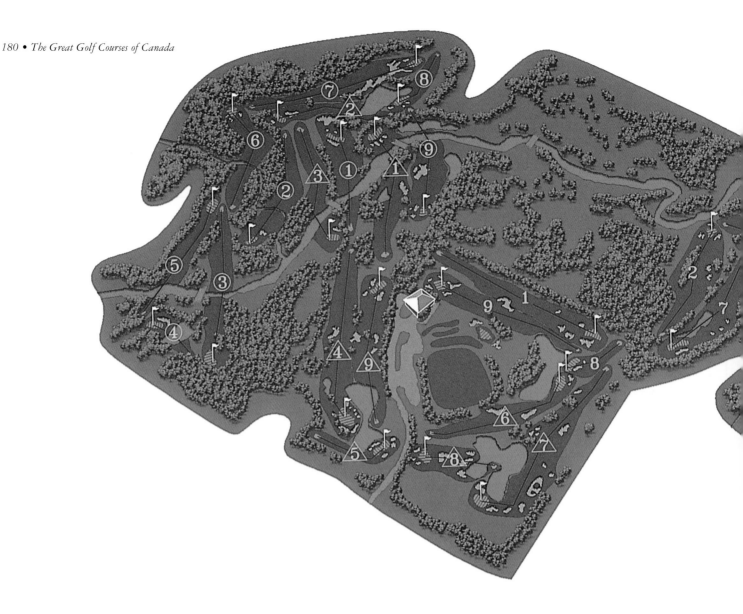

Those comments are music to the ears of the force behind Lionhead, Ignat (Iggy) Kaneff, president of Kaneff Properties Ltd. "We want to be recognized as the best golf facility in Canada," he said when Lionhead opened.

"Our immediate goal is to become the top-ranked course in Canada," says head professional Chuck Lorimer. "We're simply approaching it in a different way. We want to be thought of as a special event, much like attending a Blue Jays game or going to the Molson Indy. Everything we do here is first-class and I believe our reputation is becoming an incentive for people to want to come here. It's not inexpensive, but it's good value for your entertainment dollar.

"One of our major targets is corporate entertainment. What could be better than entertaining clients at a golf course that has an elegant atmosphere? We put great emphasis on service. All our employees take special seminars that make them sensitive to our customers' every need. We make people want to come back to Lionhead —

not just because we have a fabulous golf course, but because they are treated royally."

The royal treatment, akin to that at elite private clubs, begins when you turn off Mississauga Road about five kilometres north of Highway 401 into Lionhead's entrance. An attendant in the gatehouse bids you to stop, checks to ensure you have a tee time and then welcomes you. As you pull into the parking lot, a valet comes to get your bag and chauffeur you to the 40,000-square-·foot clubhouse.

The clubhouse is the hub of Lionhead and was designed to ensure every golfer, whether part of a corporate outing or out as a single, is treated as a pampered guest. Four locker rooms, five dining rooms, three lounges and an excellent pro shop, all served by courteous staff, provide enough amenities for even the most demanding customer.

After checking in at the clubhouse, the visitor walks 100 yards to one of the best practice facilities at any club, private or public. Covering almost three acres, it fea-

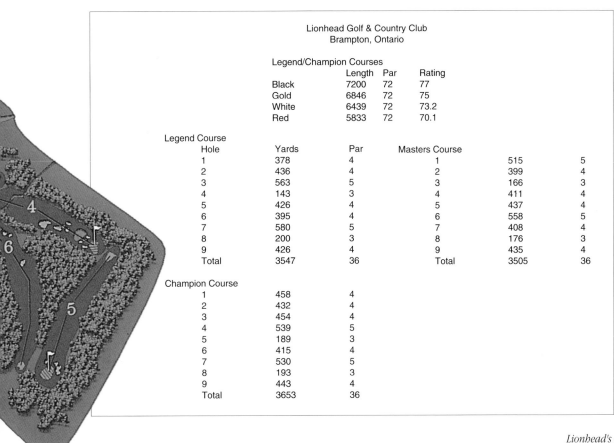

Lionhead Golf & Country Club
Brampton, Ontario

Legend/Champion Courses

	Length	Par	Rating
Black	7200	72	77
Gold	6846	72	75
White	6439	72	73.2
Red	5833	72	70.1

Legend Course Hole	Yards	Par	Masters Course	Yards	Par
1	378	4	1	515	5
2	436	4	2	399	4
3	563	5	3	166	3
4	143	3	4	411	4
5	426	4	5	437	4
6	395	4	6	558	5
7	580	5	7	408	4
8	200	3	8	176	3
9	426	4	9	435	4
Total	3547	36	Total	3505	36

Champion Course	Yards	Par
1	458	4
2	432	4
3	454	4
4	539	5
5	189	3
6	415	4
7	530	5
8	193	3
9	443	4
Total	3653	36

Lionhead's dual personality: a view from the tablelands down to the river valley.

tures turf tees, two large putting and chipping greens, and a practice bunker.

The course at Lionhead built its reputation on 27 holes, composed of three very different nines: the Masters, Legends and Champions. Each played to a par of 36 and each was about 3,600 yards from the back tees.

The Masters featured forests, wooded ravines and steeply rolling terrain demanding strategic play. The Legends was located in a valley crossing the Credit River four times, with wetlands, ponds and woods coming into play. The Champions opened with a truly spectacular first tee perched high on the bluffs, hitting down into the valley. Two other holes were played on river meadows before heading up to the tablelands with their earthen berms and ponds.

Open to the public, Lionhead's conditioning challenges that of the best private courses.

Lionhead Hosts Skins Tournament

Veteran PGA Tour pro Dave Barr from Richmond, B.C., made the best of the Cadillac Classic skins tournament held in Canada from 1989 through 1991, collecting a total of $299,00 while winning all three events. In the final edition,

held at Lionhead in August 1991, Barr gave an early indication of what was to come, landing his approach shot on the first hole less than an inch from the cup. Unfortunately, Fuzzy Zoeller also made a birdie and the money carried over to the third hole, a par 5 where Fuzzy made another birdie for $15,000. Arnold Palmer chipped in on the sixth for $10,000. Peter Jacobsen's par on the ninth was worth $20,000. On the back nine, Barr birdied the 10th, 12th, 13th and 15th holes. All but the one on 13 were for skins which brought his total to $85,000. Jacobsen (shown at right) collected $15,000 with an eagle on 16 and Barr's two-foot putt on 18 lipped out to give Zoeller $50,000

However, as previously mentioned, Lionhead is nothing if not forward looking. As of mid-1993, a new nine will be complete and the entire course will be realigned into two 18s: the Masters and the Legends. The Masters, an "Arizona-style layout" according to Lorimer, will feature moguls and mounding on the tablelands above the river valley. It will incorporate the existing Masters nine, three new holes and holes 4 to 9 of the old Champions. The new Legends will be an extremely impressive championship layout, located entirely in the valley. It will be comprised of three holes of the old Champions, six new holes and the existing Legends nine.

The presence of the Credit River gives the magnificently difficult Legends its diabolical character. Water figured into the design of every single hole on the old Legends nine.

However, the proximity of the river and its integration into the course design posed significant challenges for the developers and architect Ted Baker. No less than one year of study of the fauna and flora was required. Working closely with the Credit Valley Conservation Authority, many of the trees were preserved with careful planning and one Manitoba maple, unique to the property, was saved by constructing an island in the centre of one of the main irrigation ponds.

"Great care has been taken to preserve the natural beauty of the meadows, forests and natural foliage of the land on which Lionhead has been developed," Kaneff explains.

One would expect nothing less from Lionhead and its impressive people, no more than anyone doubts their sincere desire to become "the finest golf facility in Canada."

The scenic Credit River winds its way through the heart of the Mississaugua Golf and Country Club.

MISSISSAUGUA

Golf and Country Club

Architect: George Cumming
Head Professional: Gar Hamilton
Manager: Walter Haselsteiner
Superintendent: Paul White

Rarely in the course of any human endeavor is there one such single symbolic moment as is evident in the founding of the Mississaugua Golf and Country Club.

As recounted in the club's history, written to salute its 75th anniversary in 1981, the scene was set when a group of enthusiastic members of the Highlands Golf Club, which was about to fall victim to development, were travelling in a surrey down a dirt road which paralleled the Credit River west of Toronto. It was the autumn of 1905 and their mission was to find a new golfing home well removed from the city.

"The day was warm and the road was dusty," the chronicle notes. "When the men spotted a couple of fruit trees, they halted the surrey to pick some apples. On impulse, John Hall jumped a low fence and strode across a broad meadow. He gazed in astonishment at the beautiful scene down the valley, then turned to his friends and shouted, 'We've found it!'

" 'Found what?' they shouted back. 'Why, our golf course, of course!' Hall replied.

"Hall returned to the surrey and, impulsively pulling a golf club from his bag, picked up a ball and went back to the top of the

The 417-yard par four 8th hole features a tight green protected by sand and trees.

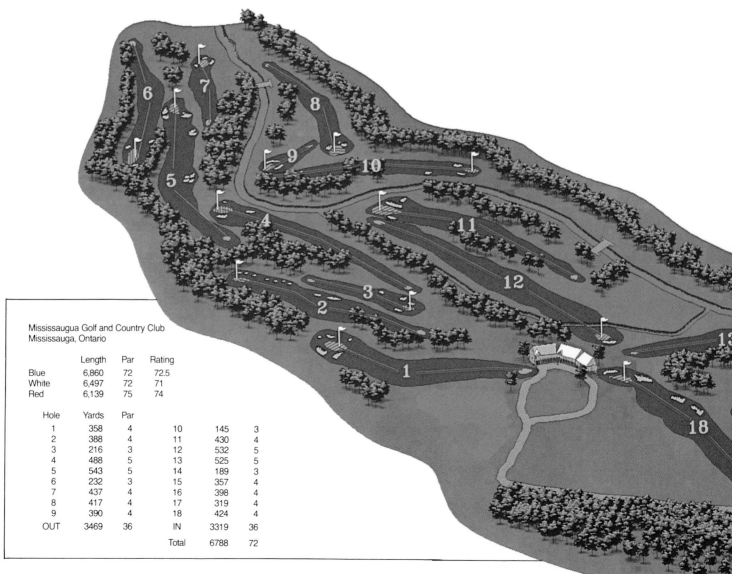

Mississaugua Golf and Country Club
Mississauga, Ontario

	Length	Par	Rating
Blue	6,860	72	72.5
White	6,497	72	71
Red	6,139	75	74

Hole	Yards	Par			
1	358	4	10	145	3
2	388	4	11	430	4
3	216	3	12	532	5
4	488	5	13	525	5
5	543	5	14	189	3
6	232	3	15	357	4
7	437	4	16	398	4
8	417	4	17	319	4
9	390	4	18	424	4
OUT	3469	36	IN	3319	36
			Total	6788	72

hill. He teed up, swung his brassie and drove the ball far into the valley below."

With such fervor, moulded in the heat generated by the discovery of such an awesome setting, the founders overlooked such picayune details as the fact that the course was all but inaccessible to the transportation modes of that era and that a wealthy, enthusiastic membership had to be raised. All such apparent obstacles were successfully dealt with in turn.

The club was extremely fortunate in having as its first president, Lauchlan Alexander Hamilton, land commissioner of the Canadian Pacific Railway. Among his feats was the surveying and laying out of the city of Vancouver. The club archives make this assessment: "He laid out the City of Vancouver and then devoted the rest of his career to the making of the Mississaugua Golf Club." Hamilton was president for 10 years and, by the time he retired, the lovely Tudor-style clubhouse had been completed and the club was settled and prosperous.

George Cumming, the noted professional at the Toronto Golf Club and 1905 Canadian Open champion, was responsible for Mississaugua's initial layout in 1906 with the assistance of Percy Barrett, professional at Toronto's Lambton club. In 1909, Cumming was commissioned to revamp the course. Famed architect Donald Ross of Dornoch, Scotland, and Pinehurst, North Carolina, toured the course 10 years later, making recommendations to change bunkering and lengthen holes. Thus, by 1923, the course had been all but rebuilt. Apart from changes in 1928, 1958 and the late 1980s, the course has not changed sub-

stantially since. From its opening holes on the bluffs overlooking the serpentine Credit River, it swoops down into the valley where John Hall drove his ball in 1905. Snaking along the valley, it loops back and forth across the river before wending its way back up the precipitous bank.

Mississaugua's physical attributes are as enviable as the unequalled calibre of its membership. In its early years, it was home to "Canada's premier golfing family" — the Thompson brothers. Bill, Stanley and Frank were the Mississaugua contingent of the five brothers. Nicol was the eldest, a professional who played out of the Hamilton Golf and Country Club in nearby Ancaster, Ontario. Matt lived and worked in the golf trade in Manitoba. The first record of their achievements came in 1919 when the three amateurs finished one, two and three in the first Toronto and District Golf Tournament to be held after the war. Frank and Bill went on to capture many tournaments including national amateur titles. Stanley, while a formidable player, would make his mark as one of the most esteemed golf course architects in the world. Indeed, he would redesign and lengthen the Mississaugua course in later years.

Although several Toronto-area courses can make a legitimate claim to Ada Mackenzie, this Canadian golfing legend took up the game by hitting balls at the Mississaugua course at the age of 17. Both during and after her time at Mississaugua, she would make an indelible mark on the game in this country, leading to her induction into the Canadian Golf Hall of Fame. When she died in 1973 at the age of 81, Ada Mackenzie had won almost every major tournament at home and abroad, including five Canadian Ladies' Opens and five Canadian Close championships, eight Canadian Ladies' Seniors Golf Association Championships and two Ontario Seniors titles. In 1933, she won every major ladies' golf championship in Canada and was named the outstanding female athlete in the country.

Tradition is a Mississaugua byword, and no mention of the club would be complete without discussing the contribution of Gordon Brydson, head professional from 1932 to 1971 and an honorary life member since. He was a fine tournament player, winning the Canadian PGA Championship, two Ontario Opens and the Quebec Open, but it is for his unstinting contribution to the life of "his" club that he is revered. "Mississaugua has been my second home," he has said. And the sentiment is reciprocated, as one longtime member stated

Hole #12: 532 yards par 5

The Big Chief Factor

In addition to numerous other tournaments, Mississaugua Golf and Country Club has played host to six Canadian Open Championships: 1931 (Walter Hagen), 1938 (Sam Snead), 1942 (Craig Wood), 1951 (Jim Ferrier), 1965 (Gene Littler) and 1974 (Bobby Nichols). It is safe to say that in every tournament round, the par-five 12th hole, nicknamed the Big Chief, has played a role. It was the site of spectacular play in 1938 during a playoff between eventual winner Sam Snead and Harry Cooper. Snead's second shot was a five-wood which hit a spectator and bounced onto the green, 35 feet from the hole. Cooper was off the green in two and chipped to 25 feet. Snead, trailing by one shot, putted for his eagle while Cooper rolled in the birdie putt. In 1965, Jack Nicklaus came to grief on this hole when his second shot cleared the river, but came to rest on the side of the plateau on which the green sits. Carding a bogey instead of an eagle or even birdie or par, it has been said, "cost Nicklaus the Open." He lost to Gene Littler by one shot in what might have been considered an omen. Of all his titles, the Canadian Open eluded Nicklaus for his entire career.

More cautious players lay up in front of the river with their second shot on the par-five 13th.

at Brydson's 80th birthday party in 1987: "Gordie has been Mississaugua; that's all there is to it."

Present Head Professional Gar Hamilton, an ideal successor to Brydson in many aspects, says Mississaugua is "an outstanding old course that is often underrated." He points to back-to-back par-fives on the back nine that typify the course's toughness.

"This course is very difficult," says Hamilton, "because it never lets up; it's relentless. The middle of the course is key to a good scoring round. Number 12 is an old hole, the par-five Big Chief. The temptation there is to go for the green in two, but you've got to hit your second shot to a small, elevated green over the river. Not a high-percentage shot for most players . . .

"The 13th is a very difficult par-five as well.

The fairway slopes quite a bit, leaving a small landing area if you want to try to get home with two shots. You'll need two absolutely perfect shots to get home here; anything less leaves you with a poor lie. In fact, many players lay up in front of the river on their second shot, just to make sure."

By the way, if you're wondering why the golf club's name is spelled differently than the city's name, there's no good reason, says the club's history. In the 1940s, "the club changed the spelling of its name from Mississauga (which corresponded with both the name of the Mississauga Indians, whose heritage was associated with the land, and the club's address on Mississauga Road) to Mississaugua, which corresponds, historically, with nothing at all." No one has been able to determine the logic behind the change in the years since.

No. 10, a short par-three, requires hitting over the Credit River, a recurring hazard at Mississaugua.

A small lake guards the 17th and 18th fairways, making the National's finishing holes among the most difficult in Canada.

THE NATIONAL

Golf Club

Architects: Tom and George Fazio
Director of Golf: Ben Kern
Superintendent: John Cherry

The National. To those who know this course, consistently rated the toughest in Canada, no two words inspire the same respect or, in some cases, fear.

The National Golf Club was opened in 1974, the culmination of a dream held by businessman Gil Blechman. "I wanted to build the best course in the world; a U.S. Open-type course," Blechman says. He enlisted Tom and George Fazio, two of the world's premier course architects, to build the best possible layout on the 400 acres he had assembled in the rolling hills north of Woodbridge, Ontario.

They were more than equal to the task. Lee Trevino, who won the 1979 Canadian Professional Golfers' Association Championship here, still calls it one of his favorite courses in the world. It is a note of distinction for The National that Trevino's winning score was 285 — one over par. Perhaps the one true mark of a great course is that it is never humbled; not even by the best.

"Everyone always talks about how difficult and hard the golf course is," says Blechman, who sold the course to the members in 1987, "but it is only the odd person who really appreciates its terrible beauty. You literally get seduced going around the bend from No. 10 to No. 13, and it's continually building to a crescendo until you come to 17 and 18."

It has been said that the first three holes of The National lure the unwary, the unprepared and the high-handicapper into a false sense of security. The opening tee shot is invited down a comfortably sloped fairway; if you stay slightly left off the tee, hitting the well-protected green should be only a short-iron situation. The second hole is a straightaway par-four, and the third another downhill par-four with an emphasis on the second shot into a green guarded on the left by a pond and on the right by bunkers. The good player may well be at even par when stepping onto the fourth tee. A humbling experience awaits.

The fourth hole is the toughest on the course, a tortuous par-five that may send the wayward hitter to the fifth tee smarting from a double-bogey. And that is just a glimpse of what lies ahead. The next hole, the first par-three you encounter, is 180 yards from the blue tees, generally into the wind to a green encircled by bunkers. Err to the left, since a slice will route your ball down a hillside and onto the fourth fairway.

As windswept and open as the front nine may be, the trip home is shorter, narrower, heavily wooded, and sports water in play on all nine holes. A river valley some 100 feet lower than the front nine provides the routing for some of the most difficult holes in Canada. Your initiation to the back nine is dramatic. The tee for the par-three 10th hole is high on a bluff, while the green awaits in the valley far below. Club selection and a smooth swing are vital here, since danger lurks in the form of rough in front, a pond right and a huge

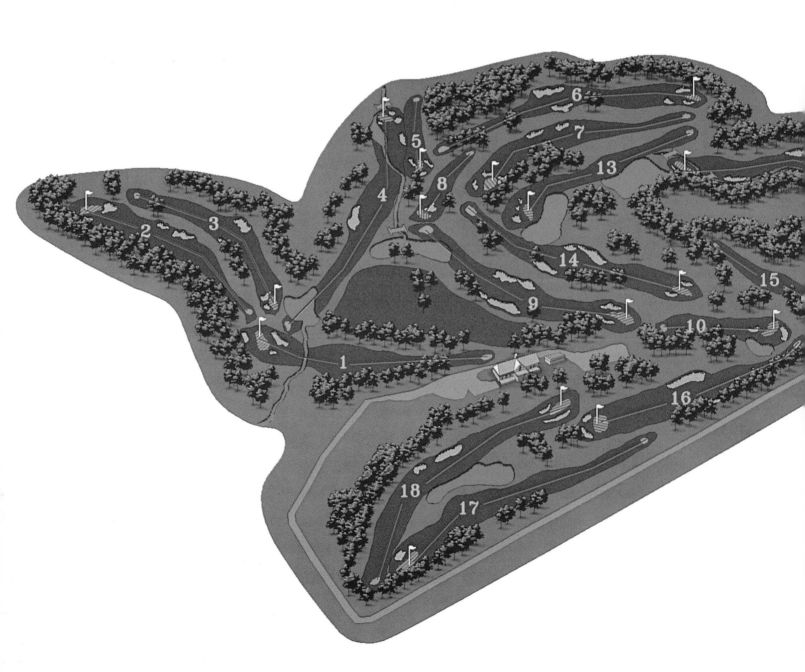

The par-three 10th marks the beginning of some of Canada's most challenging golf holes.

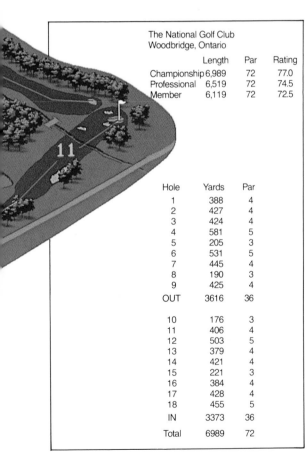

The National Golf Club Woodbridge, Ontario			
	Length	Par	Rating
Championship	6,989	72	77.0
Professional	6,519	72	74.5
Member	6,119	72	72.5

Hole	Yards	Par
1	388	4
2	427	4
3	424	4
4	581	5
5	205	3
6	531	5
7	445	4
8	190	3
9	425	4
OUT	3616	36
10	176	3
11	406	4
12	503	5
13	379	4
14	421	4
15	221	3
16	384	4
17	428	4
18	455	5
IN	3373	36
Total	6989	72

overhanging willow left.

The 11th hole provides no time to gather your wits, representing what must be one of the best par-fours in Canada. Hitting a long straight drive between bunkers right, and a hillside of tangled rough on the left, leaves a short- to mid-iron over a narrow creek into a large, undulating green. Keep in mind that the greenside rough at the National is akin to that at the U.S. Open, just the way Blechman wanted it.

Don't even consider cutting the corner on the next hole, a 500-yard, double-dogleg par-five, since accomplishing that near-impossible feat would involve carrying a stand of towering pine trees. Respect this as a true three-shot hole, laying up on your second effort. The river describes the left boundary of this beauty until it slashes across the fairway just in front of the sinister, multi-leveled green. A par on this hole is a badge of honor to be displayed with pride once back in the safe confines of the clubhouse.

Number 13 provides no respite: a 360-yard par-four that requires a drive to avoid a lake and creek on the left and ruggedly inclined rough on the right. The second shot on the dogleg-left requires a short iron to a small, well-bunkered green perched beside another pond.

No mention of The National would be complete without description of the greens. Slick, treacherous, subtle, undulating: words can scarcely hint at the work that is left once the ball reaches the putting surface. The 16th hole, perhaps one of the least remarkable in terms of design, attains mythical stature within the golfing brotherhood on the merits of its green alone. Being above the hole could mean chipping back onto the green with your next shot.

The view from the highly elevated 18th tee at The National provides seldom-equalled scenic serenity. Standing in a chute formed by tall, straight pines, you survey a good portion of the course. A clear lake on the right provides a sense of tranquil beauty but, as is The National's mischievious wont, also taunts the player to cut off as much water as he dares on his tee shot on the 445-yard uphill par-five. Overly cautious hitters will find themselves in bunkers left, blocked from the green by weeping willows. The approach shot must be high and soft to ensure the ball doesn't skid over the green into what can only be characterized as wildlife habitat.

And so it goes. The unforgiving, unforgettable National demands respect. Intelligent shot selection and a smooth swing will permit not only survival, but enjoyment.

Playing The National may not be the only way to see the course. Director of Golf Ben Kern says there are viewing areas on the course for up to 50,000 spectators and the membership is receptive to hosting the right event. "The Canadian Open, of course, the World Cup or some other significant international event would be appropriate," says the former PGA Tour player. "We have a great course and a great event would certainly showcase what we have hidden here."

Thought by many to be the toughest hole on the course, the par-four 11th rewards only two perfect shots.

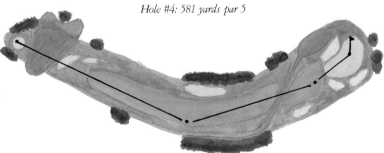

Hole #4: 581 yards par 5

Small, fast and well-protected greens are par for the National.

Most Difficult Hole

Number 4 (581 yards, par-five) A tight, twisting double dogleg that severely punishes an errant tee shot. A meandering creek bordering dense rough lurks on the right while enormous bunkers and overhanging willow trees defend the left. The creek winds across the fairway at the 150-yard mark and continues down the left side, threatening a wayward second shot. A long but narrow green is encircled by expansive bunkers, enticing the player to lay up short of the green and offer a birdie opportunity as a reward to a precise wedge.

Osprey Valley is a heathlands course, which can be loosely described as an inland links. On the 10th hole, you can see the links influence, punctuated with a pond and trees.

OSPREY VALLEY

Heathlands Golf Course

Public

What is a "heathlands course"? "It's an inland links," says course designer Doug Carrick of Toronto. "Although Osprey Valley might be considered more of a links style, because we shaped dunes and mounds to make it resemble a seaside course." Enhancing that emulation is the sheep's fescue grass which, as it ripples in Osprey Valley's ever-present wind, reminds you of Ireland.

And that's not surprising, because Carrick is a diligent student of the game who learned his trade under Robbie Robinson, one of Stanley Thompson's disciples. He has made pilgrimages to Britain to play the true links courses, taking photographs and trying to learn what makes them great. "I really studied them before taking on the Osprey project. I tried to emulate some of the characteristics of those courses, especially around the greens; all the little hollows and different types of shots you get over there, bump and run, and that sort of thing.

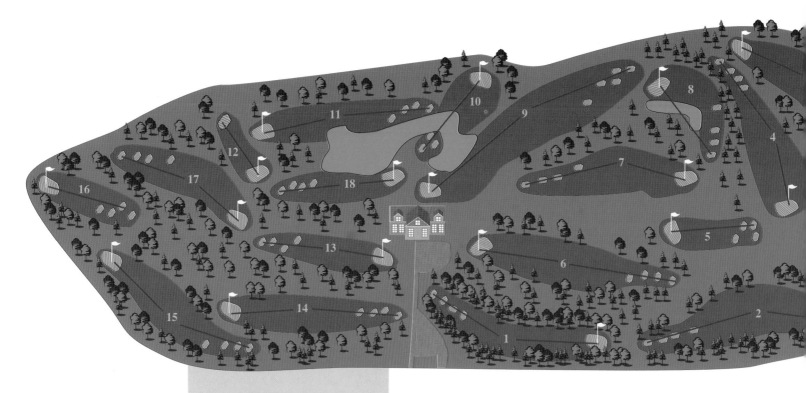

Osprey Valley Heathlands Golf Course
Alton, Ontario

	Length	Par
Black	6810	71
Blue	6423	71

Hole	Yards	Par
1	515	4
2	389	3
3	411	5
4	367	4
5	205	4
6	451	3
7	424	4
8	156	5
9	553	4
OUT	3471	36
10	159	3
11	561	5
12	174	3
13	443	5
14	527	4
15	412	4
16	196	4
17	449	3
18	418	4
IN	3339	35
Total	6810	71

"A lot of modern designs take the ground game out of golf," Carrick observes. "And that has a lot to do with over-maintenance. At Osprey, they don't over-water the golf course. They keep it relatively dry and that's good because then it plays more like a links experience. And the wind always blows." That wind more often hinders than helps at Osprey Valley, which does not have a weak hole among its 18. It is, as the architect says, "a good, strong, walkable golf course."

The first hole, a shortish par 5, dares the player to carry the cross-bunkers in the dogleg. Hitting a crisp approach through the gap in the fence, avoiding the grassy hollows and bunkers, starts the round off with a birdie. Cross-bunkers also come into play on the par-4 second hole, as well as a number of others. As in most Carrick designs, players attacking the line over these bunkers will be rewarded with a more advantageous approach angle.

The wind makes the long, par-3 fifth hole even longer than it says on the card. "This is a tough hole, with the wind, the bunkers on the right side, grassy hollows on the left, and mounds wrapping around the green," says Carrick. No. 6 is a "bear of a par 4," the architect says. There are no bunkers, which is only fair since this hole plays right into the teeth of the wind. "It's a test of power. You can roll the ball on to the green, but you have to roll it through a swale."

The par-5 ninth hole is a double dogleg where you must hit the green or face dire consequences. A creek runs down the right side of the fairway before emptying into a pond, and the challenge is to cut off as much of the creek as you dare on the tee shot. There are a couple of choices on the second shot: play way to the left, over some bunkers cut into a dune, or play far to the right and face a longer approach over water to a well-bunkered elevated green. "Very

rarely does anyone hit this green in two," says Carrick. "That's quite a feat."

Unlike a true links course, Osprey Valley does feature some ponds. The tee shot on the par-5 11th must carry water before heading down a valley, threading through a series of bunkers. Bunkers also tantalize the second shot, and there's one more sandpit right in front of the green. As at many green sites at this course, grassy hollows are popular hazards on this hole. They are plentiful as well on the next hole, a mid-iron par 3 nestled into the dunes. Although greens here are not overly spacious, club selection on this hole is important, since there could be a two-club difference depending on the pin position.

A dual-tiered fairway offers options on the second shot on the straightaway, par-5 14th hole, which is bracketed by dunes. "You have the choice to go up, or down to the right below some crossbunkers," Carrick says. "The ideal line is to hit it

The par-5 11th hole requires power and accuracy. First you must carry the water, then thread your way through bunkers before even thinking about hitting the green.

The fifth hole at Osprey Valley features an ancient stone fence, fescue, and British-influenced bunkering styles. They combine to create a very tough par 3.

over the cross-bunkers which, if you are a long hitter, will put you on the green in two or leave an easy chip. If you bail out, you have to fly it over some deep pot bunkers. Risk and reward, right?"

As on other holes here, an ancient stone fence adds character to the par-4 15th. The best line off the tee is down the right side, just over the tip of the amoeba-shaped waste bunker. You can roll the ball onto the par-3 16th, but make sure you arrive at the right terrace of the three-tiered green to guarantee par. After surviving the 17th, another "bear of a par 4," according to the architect, your round concludes with an elegant par 4. A following wind will assist you in carrying the three cross-bunkers.

Aficionados of Osprey Valley will be thrilled to learn that it will have two dis-

tinctive siblings opening for play in the year 2000. The south course, some of it built on a former gravel quarry, will be a sand wasteland course "à la Pine Valley," says Carrick. It will wind through natural ponds and a pine plantation; about 3,000 trees have been transplanted to enhance the routing. The north course will be more of a traditional parkland course.

The eventual 54-hole public facility an hour northwest of Toronto is intended to be the centrepiece of a conference centre, golf villas and resort owned by developer Jerry Humeniuk. Humeniuk is also considering an 18-hole short course for beginners, juniors, families and instruction. It promises to be a complex unique in Canada.

Don't be misled by Doug Carrick's self-deprecating manner. The Toronto architect's portfolio includes note-worthy projects from one side of Canada to the other: Angus Glen, King Valley, and Greystone, all in Ontario; Twin Rivers in Newfoundland; and the new Greywolf course in Panorama, British Columbia. He has also completed a showpiece project in Austria for Frank Stronach, founder of auto parts giant Magna International, and is working on another Magna course in Aurora, Ontario.

A longtime member of the American Society of Golf Course Architects, Carrick says his design philosophy centres on playability. "That's one of the most important aspects of what I take from one project to another. A second aspect would be strategy, in terms of making people think of how they are going to attack every hole, on every shot. I always try to provide a balance of shotmaking throughout the course, making sure that there's a good chance that most players will have to use every club in their bag. I try not to favour one type of shot, so that there's a mix of draws and fades, although that's sometimes tough to do. The other thing that's important to me is to avoid lay-up shots off the tee and blind shots."

Block out the trees on the par-4 15th, focus just on the stone fence, fescue, and bunkers, and you would swear you are in Ireland.

Secluded in rural southwestern Ontario, Redtail Golf Course is a hidden gem, the dream of two wealthy diehard golfers.

REDTAIL

Golf Course

Private

Redtail Golf Course. Near London. Owned by two — well, maybe *eccentric* is too strong a word — eclectic millionaires. Designed by Donald Steel of Hillingdon, England. Quaint cottages for overnight accommodation. An exquisite Tudor-style clubhouse.

Sounds like it should be in Britain, doesn't it? And it would fit in over there, quite comfortably. Queen Elizabeth and Prince Philip agreed when they reportedly stayed there a few years back. Scottish actor Sean Connery loves it more each time he visits.

The result of a dream concocted by Chris Goodwin and John Drake, Redtail has been raved about by those fortunate enough to be allowed to play it since it opened in 1992. George Peper, editor of *Golf Magazine*, says the green speeds approach "Mach 1," and Tom Doak, architecture editor for the same publication, says Redtail is "one of the most perfect golf operations I've seen."

Doak, himself a course architect, devotes considerable space

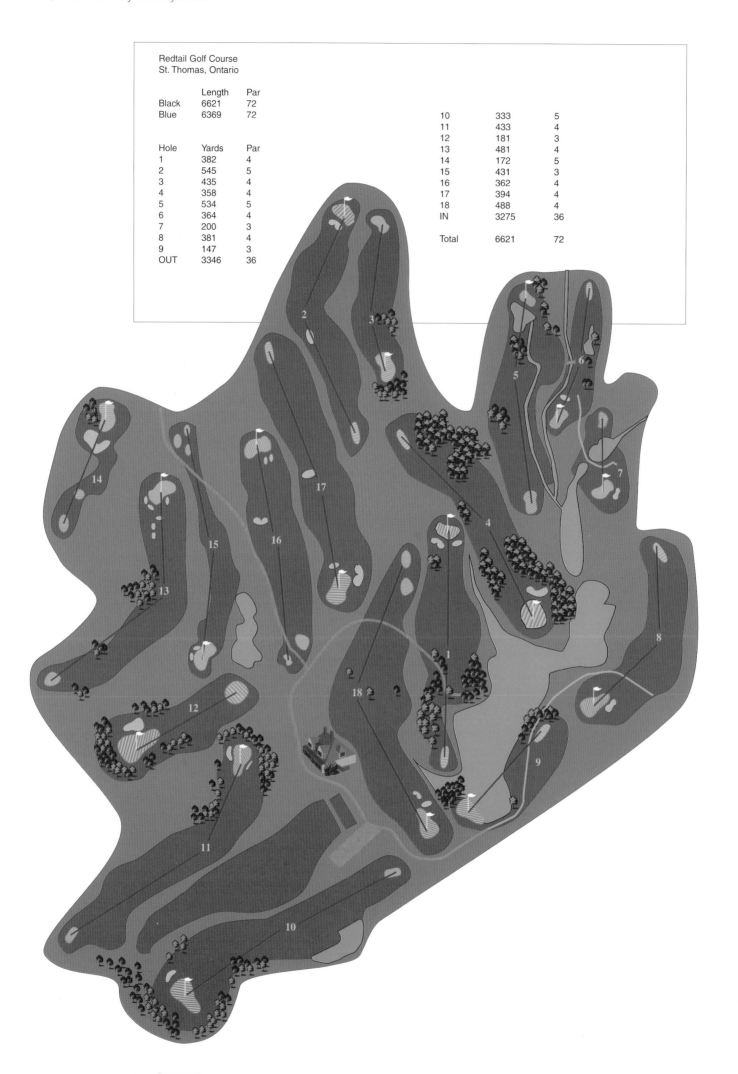

Redtail Golf Course
St. Thomas, Ontario

	Length	Par
Black	6621	72
Blue	6369	72

Hole	Yards	Par
1	382	4
2	545	5
3	435	4
4	358	4
5	534	5
6	364	4
7	200	3
8	381	4
9	147	3
OUT	3346	36

Hole	Yards	Par
10	333	5
11	433	4
12	181	3
13	481	4
14	172	5
15	431	3
16	362	4
17	394	4
18	488	4
IN	3275	36
Total	6621	72

"Bruiser" is the name of the brawny 442-yard third hole. It represents the strategic philosophy of Donald Steel's elemental design: the most advantageous angle to the green is attainable only by successfully taking the riskiest path with your tee shot.

to Redtail in his book, *The Confidential Guide to Golf Courses*: "My favourite aspect of the course is the greens contouring, which is among the best done in my lifetime." A *Golf Magazine* ranking panel called it a "hidden gem," no doubt due in large part to the cheerleading led by Canadian golf writer Lorne Rubenstein, an honorary member of Redtail's "Roundtable." Rubenstein says this could become Canada's Pine Valley and that it certainly should be ranked among the top 100 courses in the world.

The manner in which Redtail came to be is antithetical to almost very accepted modern practice of developing, designing, building, and operating a golf course. Drake and Goodwin were devout golfers who had played just about everywhere around the globe. Rather than being bowled over by the wretched excesses evident in many new course concepts, they found themselves drawn back to the game's basics. Their goal was to emulate the fundamental strengths of golf, not to embellish them.

They purchased 210 acres of rolling property that had been a horse farm, its pastures dotted with stands of deciduous trees and bisected by winding valleys. They happened upon Steel's name in a casual conversation with a golfing buddy in the Bahamas. When they contacted the architect in 1989, he had never done a project in North America.

Despite that, Steel and his assistant Tom Mackenzie were the ideal choice to design this unique course for the idiosyncratic duo of wealthy businessmen from nearby London, Ontario. "I never belonged to the school that believed you needed to move Heaven and earth," said Steel, who, in addition to designing courses, was the golf correspondent for the *London Sunday Telegraph* until 1990. Although some earth was moved to create this golfing Heaven, it was minimal; just over 50,000 cubic yards were pushed around on Redtail, the same

For the fortunate few who get to play a round at Redtail, their rare experience commences with a 387-yard par 4 called Funnel, for obvious reasons.

amount often moved on a single hole of a typical modern course.

"The land at Redtail was perfect for the creation of the Drake-Goodwin dream, which was to create a private golf course and an exhaustive test of golfing ability," Steel said to commemorate the opening of the course. "The dramatic wooded ravines and the steeply undulating ground could not have been better to design such a course, in keeping with our philosophy of always striving to move the minimum earth and to blend in with what is there already.

"The brief from Drake and Goodwin was clear, and that was that 'following from Cypress Point and Pine Valley, our green areas will be extremely challenging, almost to the point of being unfair: A great deal of undulation and very, very fast.' The style of course which they envisaged matched our own in that 'we would prefer a design that preserves the natural features of the property, bordering almost on the wild.' They were equally certain that there should be no constraints which would compromise the golf."

Steel's design, driven by the vision of Goodwin and Drake, proves that perfection can be achieved through restraint. The design is elegant in its minimalism, which is also a credit to the founders, who located property ideal for the purpose. There are only 34 bunkers on the par-72, 6,700-yard course, and the fairways, while relatively narrow, never offer less than a perfect lie.

Minimalism is also apparent in the costs to build and operate this jewel, which cost only $2.1 million to build, exclusive of irrigation. Steel's fee was about a tenth of that, and the annual maintenance budget is less than $400,000.

Redtail has been called the most private course in North America. There are no members, unless you want to categorize Drake and Goodwin as such. Instead, there is the Roundtable, a group of select individuals who pay a fee for the privilege to be part of this incredible golfing experience. Apparently, you do not ask to become a Roundtable member; you must be invited.

How do you get on Redtail? An introduction by a Roundtable member would help. Being a "keen golfer" is essential.

Redtail: After finding Redtail — a tough task, tucked as it is in the backwaters of Southwestern Ontario's farmland — and getting on the ultra-private course — an even tougher assignment — your golf game will face a significant challenge. The owners wanted a player's course and that's what English architect Donald Steel gave them. The 11th hole, deceptively called "Bluebird", is the No. 1 handicap hole. At only 415 yards from the tips, it calls for precise shotmaking and superb putting — Redtail in microcosm.

At only 354 yards, the sixth hole doesn't present a difficult tee shot. The challenge comes when confronted by the approach to a perched green: Do you fly it in with a precise short iron, or try to run it in past the front bunker?

But don't hold your breath. Rarely are there more than 50 golfers on the course on any given day. Drake and Goodwin keep it that way so their baby is always in pristine condition.

Redtail, like the Pine Valley layout it aspires to emulate in some ways, is tough. There are only two sets of tees (appropriately called "black" and "blue") and the mid- to high-handicapper is in for a long day.

But, oh, what a day that would be!

Toronto, Ontario

ST. GEORGE'S

Golf and Country Club

Architect: Stanley Thompson
Head Professional: Neil Verwey
Manager: Patricia Mann
Superintendent: John Gall

The seclusion of St. George's Golf and Country Club, an oasis of calm tucked out of sight near one of Toronto busiest thoroughfares, represents in many ways the sum of all that is wonderful about golf. Ironically, St. George's owes its beginnings to Toronto's bustling atmosphere: it was originally opened to provide recreation for guests at the city's then-remarkable Royal York Hotel. The course was called the Royal York Golf Club from its inception in 1928 until 1946, when its financial arrangement ended with the Canadian Pacific Railway, owners of the hotel.

Astutely, the founders invited Stanley Thompson of Toronto, recognized as one of the premier course architects in the world at the time, to design 18 holes on the convoluted, heavily treed acreage. Thompson fulfilled his mandate admirably, producing a layout that has stood the test of time as very few other courses have. Head Professional Neil Verwey cites one of Thompson's commandments when he says, "The golf course fits the terrain. It doesn't have that 'manufactured' feel to it that a lot of new ones do.

"Each hole is unique unto itself," says Verwey. "There is no sameness to any of the holes at St. George's. The course is very

Stanley Thompson's classic layout has stood the test of time.

playable. The landing areas aren't tight, but you have to be very careful with your second shots and by no means are you finished once you get to the green. The par-threes here are fantastic and, of course, it has Thompson's thumbprint, which is his great fairway bunkers."

Four Canadian Opens were played on Thompson's classic layout: 1933 (won by Joe Kirkwood), 1949 (E.J. Harrison), 1960 (Art Wall) and 1968 (Bob Charles). In addition, St. George's has been a favored site for the du Maurier Ltd. Classic, designated as one of the four "major" events on the Ladies' Professional Golf Association Tour. Two-time winner JoAnne Carner (1975, 1978) says it is "the best club I have ever played; no four finer finishing holes in the world." After her second win, she commented that the final round was "the

St. George's Golf and Country Club
Toronto, Ontario

	Length	Par	Rating
Blue	6797	71	73
White	6477	71	71
Red	6205	71	69.5

Hole	Yards	Par			
1	378	4	10	377	4
2	420	4	11	517	5
3	201	3	12	383	4
4	480	5	13	214	3
5	403	4	14	446	4
6	146	3	15	580	5
7	442	4	16	203	3
8	217	3	17	447	4
9	543	5	18	400	4
OUT	3230	35	IN	3567	36
			Total	6797	71

greatest round I ever played on the toughest course I ever played." In total, St. George's played host to five du Maurier Ltd. Classics between 1975 and 1984.

Playing the course like the LPGA stars would be too much to ask, but here are a few notes from the hole-by-hole commentary prepared for the event: "The first hole is one of the finer opening holes in golf. From an elevated tee, the golfer plays to a roomy but sloping fairway. The second shot will be about 130 yards to a slightly elevated green. The prevailing wind quarters left to right. The second hole is one of the tougher holes because of the undulating terrain. The tee shot is from one elevation to another and the fairway slopes to the right. The approach will be about 180 yards to a green protected by a boundary on the left and bunkers right. The green is long and narrow, demanding precision and control from the two-iron to five-wood second shot. The third is another elevated tee shot, but the big problem here is the narrow and severely sloping green. Though the shot will be something like a three-iron, the green won't be too difficult to hit, sitting as it does so receptively below the player. But once on the green, the player will have to take care."

The finishing holes have claimed their share of competitors, the hole-by-hole commentary notes in its description of the 14th. "By now, the hills may be taking their toll on players, but anyone who can hang in there will be in good shape. Pars are the thing on these holes in the middle of the back side. Golfers will likely flirt with the left side of the fairway,

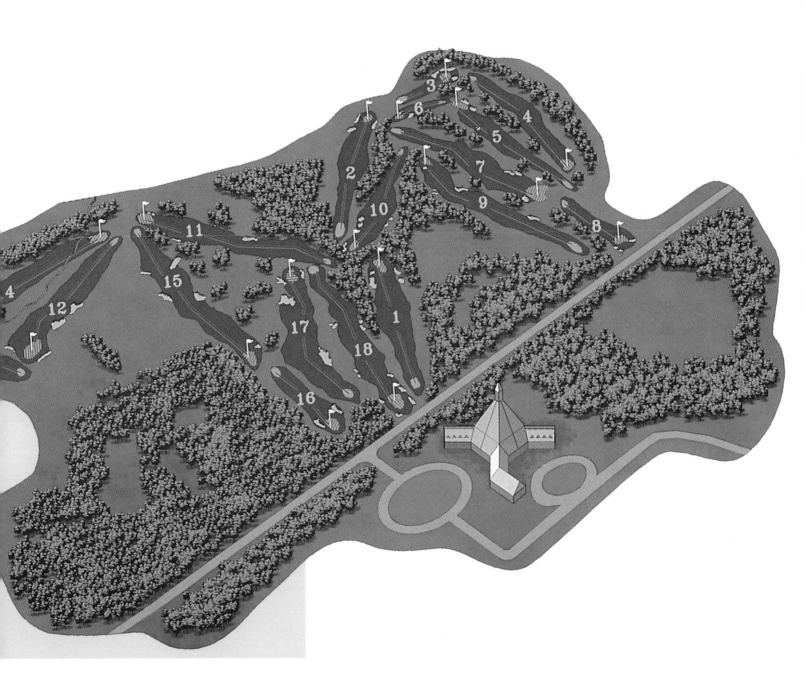

St. George's features excellent par-fours. On the 446-yard 14th, the second shot must clear the creek.

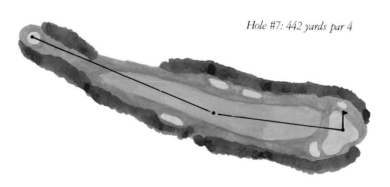

Hole #7: 442 yards par 4

The Toughest Hole at St. George's

The Number 1-rated stroke hole at St. George's Golf and Country Club is the par-four seventh hole which plays 442 yards from the blue tees and 20 yards less from the whites. Head Pro Neil Verwey respectfully suggests that you "grunt" on your tee shot. "You've got to hit the ball as far and straight as you can. Even then, you'll still be facing a long-iron or fairway wood into a very severe green. There are fairway traps and mounds all the way up the left side, and trees on both sides — and it's all uphill. Your second shot has to carry bunkers in front of the green. A super hole."

but this is the blind side from the tee. Still, those who succeed in placing their ball will have a shorter club for the second shot. It is a give-and-take hole, for the second shot from the left side will contend with a green banked on the right by a hill, and directly in line with the player's approach. The 15th is some kind of hole! After two shots down a fairway reminiscent of the first, the golfer is left with a shot up to the clouds. The green is so raised that it seems the shot is a pop fly, but it is a very difficult green to work with, angling on the front and back right.

"What a challenge these final holes are," the commentary continues. "The 16th hole takes the golfer to the perimeter of the course, not far from where she began, and offers the first of a variety of testing shots down the last stretch. Here is a green with a narrow entrance, a deep bunker right and trees left. A high fade is the shot, but that's a bit of a challenge with a long-iron. Number 17 is a slight dogleg-right where the long hitter does

have an advantage: she can try to shave yards by cutting the corner. That will leave a four- or five-iron to a well-trapped green cut on an angle. To the right is a gully and a bunker demanding a shot from eight feet down.

"Nothing like a finishing hole that leads toward a rambling old clubhouse in the distance," the summary concludes. "Victory may seem within grasp, but the approach is fraught with problems. A bunker at the left front and another at the right corner make the second shot hard on the nerves. Even if the bunkers are avoided, there is always the chance of the next being played from the sidehill lie in rough that fringes the green and bunkers. As usual, the green will be quick, and so this final hole will epitomize all that is best about St. George's as a site for a major championship: it demands the full shot mixed with the delicate touch, the knowledge to hit a variety of shots, and the good sense to know when to apply that knowledge. It demands restraint, finesse and strength."

Many championships have been decided on the 18th green: four Canadian Opens and five du Maurier Ltd. Classics among them.

*Weston is famous for its treacher-
ous greens, such as this one on
the par-four fifth hole.*

WESTON

Golf and Country Club

*Architect: Willie Park Jr.
Head Professional: Herb Holzscheiter
Manager: Michael Jory
Superintendent: Thom Charters*

The Weston Golf and Country Club is best known as the site of Arnold Palmer's first professional victory. While Palmer's win at the 1955 Canadian Open at Weston was a memorable occasion, it is not the sole reason the course is recognized as one of Canada's best.

Weston was founded in 1914 following a town-hall meeting at which local businessmen decided to rent land in the nearby Humber Valley to construct a course. Initially, they built a crude four-hole course which served as an adventurous but adequate start. The area also served as a pasture and one of the first problems was keeping grazing cattle off the greens.

With a growing membership, the course soon expanded to nine holes and Percy Barrett, who had been an assistant to the famous Harry Vardon in Britain and runner-up in the first Canadian Open in 1904, was hired as the first professional.

Barrett was a strict disciplinarian. One day, when he was about to hit his drive off the first tee, he wheeled around and pointed his finger at a caddie. "You were talking," accused Barrett. "No sir, I was not talking," the caddie boldly replied. "Well," said the gruff Barrett, "you were going to."

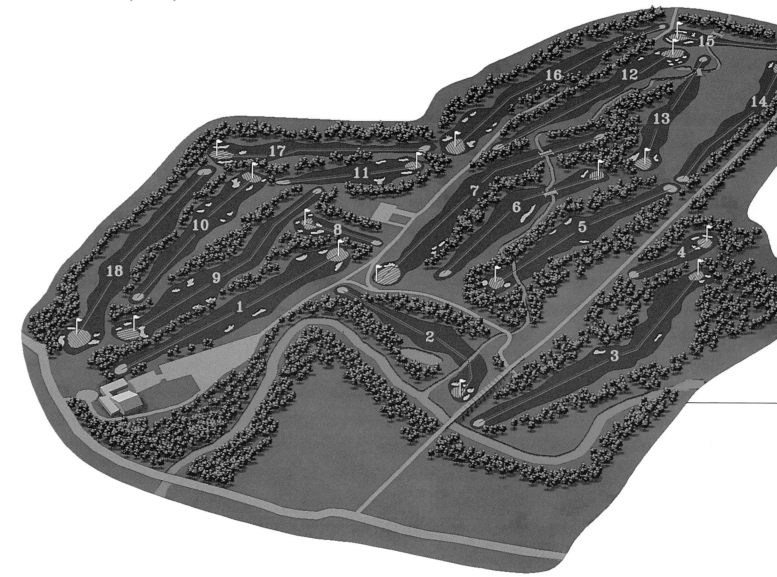

In 1921, the club purchased the land it had been renting, as well as some surrounding acreage, and hired Willie Park Jr., a noted Scottish architect who twice had won the British Open, to design an 18-hole layout. The design was well-received and, with the war over, applications for membership came in droves. The fees for 1921 were set at $60 for gentlemen and $30 for ladies. In 1922, the course was opened officially with much pomp that included an exhibition match with English professionals Sandy Taylor and Alex Herd taking on Barrett and 1905 Canadian Open champion George Cumming of the Toronto Golf Club.

While the course has remained virtually unchanged from Park's admirable original design, nature has forced a few alterations. Most of those have come at the spectacular second hole, now a 314-yard par-four that has become the course's signature. Players tee off from a precipice 120 feet above a fairway bounded on the right by a pond and on the left by

rough and trees. The green sits at the foot of a towering railway trestle which dominates the landscape.

In the past, however, this hole was a par-three, only to be destroyed by the flooding of the Humber River during Hurricane Hazel four decades ago. For a time, it became a lengthy par-four with a green on the far side of the trestle. The players' challenge was to decide whether to go under or over the ominous structure.

Anyone who plays Weston for the first time is struck by the immaculate conditioning, another trademark of the course. The 6,698-yard layout is kept in impeccable shape and possesses lightning-fast greens. In fact, veteran PGA Tour star Raymond Floyd has compared their speed with that at major championships such as The Masters. The greens are, for the most part, small and very deceiving. Scoring well at Weston requires patience and a smooth stroke on the greens.

Weston is a traditional course in every sense

Weston Golf and Country Club Weston, Ontario			
	Length	Par	Rating
Blue	6698	72	72
White	6465	72	71
Yellow	5889	74	73
Hole	Yards	Par	
1	413	4	
2	314	4	
3	472	5	
4	156	3	
5	424	4	
6	385	4	
7	571	5	
8	131	3	
9	448	4	
OUT	3314	36	
10	337	4	
11	235	3	
12	471	5	
13	376	4	
14	438	4	
15	192	3	
16	541	5	
17	350	4	
18	444	4	
IN	3384	36	
Total	6698	72	

of the word. The majority of holes are lined with maple, oak and spruce trees from tee to green, and a level stance on the fairways is a rare treat. The course ebbs and flows with many natural changes in elevation and scenery. There are no gimmicks at Weston; what you see is what you get.

A linkage of three holes — the fifth, sixth and seventh — provide one of the best tests of golf in Canada, and many a match has been won or lost here despite their early appearance in the round. The first two are long par-fours with danger lurking on both sides of their fairways. Both are remarkable for their extremely difficult greens that require precision placement of approach shots and careful study of the resulting putts. Ending up on the wrong side of the pin almost certainly assures a disastrous three-putt. The last in this tough trio is a tremendous 571-yard par-five with the tee set back in a tree-lined chute. To have any chance of reaching the green in two shots,

The eighth hole, although only 131 yards long, yields more bogies than birdies.

players must power a drive to the top of a knoll which cuts across the fairway. Being short of the crest can result in a blind second shot, the outcome being a bogey, or worse.

Weston's 18th hole presents a challenging completion to a round. A 444-yard par-four, the downhill dogleg-left plays shorter than its yardage indicates, but requires a brilliant tee shot. The green rarely holds anything but a superb approach and a bump-and-run strategy is often best. Once there, heed the members' credo that all putts break to the clubhouse, although you'll be hard pressed to do so since your eyes tend to deceive you on this subtle putting surface.

Weston has an impressive tournament history. In addition to the 1955 Canadian Open, it has played host to the 1971 Ontario Open, won by the late George Knudson, and Ontario Amateurs in 1964 and 1978, both won by Gary Cowan. In 1990, to honor its 75th anniversary, the club opened its doors to the Cadillac Classic skins game, featuring Palmer, Floyd, Mark Calcavecchia and eventual winner Dave Barr of Richmond, B.C. The year was capped by the hosting of the Canadian Amateur championship, won, fittingly, by Weston member Warren Sye.

Weston is perennially rated one of the best conditioned courses in Canada.

The 16th hole with its elevated green plays even longer than the 541 yards on the card.

Birth of a Legend

In 1955, a 25-year-old rookie professional named Arnold Palmer had his back to the wall. He had been shut out on the PGA Tour despite winning the U.S. Amateur the previous year and had enough money to last just six more weeks on tour. Coming to Weston Golf and Country Club to face a stellar field for the Canadian Open, he couldn't be blamed for feeling despondent. "I was frustrated with my play," Palmer recalls. "I felt I had been playing well, but I wasn't getting any results." But playing on a rain-soaked course that yielded low scores, Palmer sat in second place after the first round, firing a 64 to trail Charley Sifford by a shot. He improved on that standing the following day, shooting 67 to take the lead. The third round, he achieved another 64 in a curious manner: three shots that appeared headed for the woods caromed back into play after hitting spectators. At 21 under par after three rounds, Palmer coasted through the final day with a 70. The winner's cheque for $2,400 staked him on his way to becoming one of the best golfers of all time.

The Links at Crowbush Cove come by their name honestly. Perched on the north shore of Prince Edward Island, the course is a stone's throw from salt water. And the wind is incessant.

Morell, Prince Edward Island

THE LINKS AT CROWBUSH COVE

Public

In 1998, *Golf Digest* named The Links at Crowbush Cove one of the Ten Best Public Courses in North America — the only Canadian course cited in the Top Ten of the 5,300 places to play worldwide as rated by the magazine's subscribers. Astoundingly, that honour came only four years after that U.S. magazine and *SCORE*, Canada's national golf magazine, both named Crowbush Cove the best new golf course in Canada.

Or maybe it wasn't so astounding. Architect Thomas McBroom of Toronto was gratified when the government of Prince Edward Island contracted him to design a golf course on what is as close to a true linksland site as possible in these days of environmental conservancy. McBroom responded with a stunningly beautiful layout on the island's north shore that challenges even the best players in the world when the ever-present wind is up. In 1995, a Canadian Tour event had to be suspended because of a howling wind. "It was the first time we were ever 'winded' out," recalls Rob Gilroy, director of communications for the Canadian Tour. "Balls were blowing uphill on the greens. Half of the field couldn't break 80. It was unbelievable."

Right from its inception, Crowbush Cove has not been shy about standing up

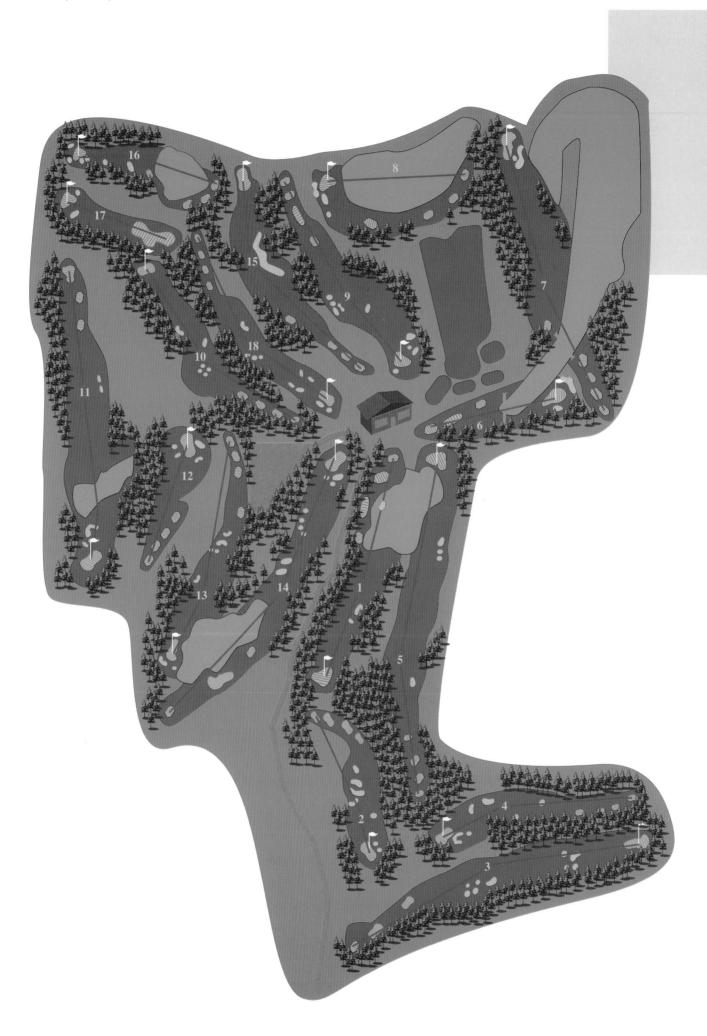

The Links at Crowbush Cove
Morell, Prince Edward Island

	Length	Par
Crows	6903	72
Blue	6475	72
White	5964	72
Red	4864	72

Hole	Yards	Par			
1	409	4	10	463	4
2	366	4	11	565	5
3	500	5	12	191	3
4	379	4	13	413	4
5	603	5	14	515	5
6	191	3	15	393	4
7	392	4	16	360	4
8	219	3	17	113	3
9	367	4	18	464	4
OUT	3426	36	IN	3477	36
			Total	7140	72

Looking back down the ninth fairway, you can see how architect Tom McBroom sought to recreate a British feel at Crowbush Cove.

to the best golfers. A year after the finest amateurs in the country tested it in the 1997 Canadian Amateur, it hosted the Export 'A' Skins Game, featuring Fred Couples, John Daly, Canadian Mike Weir, and Mark O'Meara. Although O'Meara finished second to Couples in that particular made-for-TV event, he would go on to be named the 1998 PGA Tour Player of the Year after winning two majors, The Masters and the British Open. He and Couples, particularly, were complimentary about the course.

Crowbush is a unique blend of traditional golf course design and modern construction with state-of-the-art environmental preservation techniques. This magnificent seaside layout is built on the island's famous red clay soil and winds around sensitive coastal dunes and wetlands. The 6,900-yard, par-72 course features lush bentgrass fairways, tees, and USGA greens and high-contrast white sand bunkers.

Despite the name, The Links at Crowbush Cove is actually a combination of three styles: the opening holes mean-

Holes 9 and 15 run parallel in this aerial view. Both are mid-length par 4s with the usual Crowbush hazards – wind, sand and fescue.

der through thick stands of native spruce, then there are the wetland holes and, of course, the dunes holes. The combination of water, rolling fairways, strategic bunkering, and well-guarded greens makes this a golf course that requires every club in the bag. Narrow entrances to elevated greens reward target golf and, as at any seaside course, wind is a most significant factor. The players in that 1995 Canadian Tour event can attest to that!

A round at Crowbush Cove begins with a couple of relatively benign par 4s. At 409 and 366 yards respectively, these holes allow you to sense the course's rhythm. Let there be no mistake: This course has a rhythm you must dance to or you will pay a steep price. For despite

being a tourist destination, this course is a difficult outing. You must hit the ball where the course dictates or else. The par-5 third hole is a good example. At only 500 yards from the back tees, its green is apparently begging to be reached in two. But the prudent player will resist that urge after surveying the cross bunkers 100 yards short of the green, the marsh fronting the narrow entrance to a convoluted green and the greenside bunker left. Better to lay back and deliver a well-struck third shot close to the hole.

Holes four through eight at Crowbush Cove have been likened to Pebble Beach, with some great golf holes typified by the gorgeous par-4 fourth, the brawny 600-yard fifth, the terrifying par-3 sixth with its 190-yard carry over a marsh and a pond, and the demanding 392-yard seventh. This marvelous stretch concludes with the ocean-side eighth, a 219-yard par 3 with nothing but water 'twixt tee and green. It was here, so the story goes, that the Canadian Tour players couldn't hit the green even with drivers in that gale-force wind.

The par-3 17th has generated a lot of controversy, with supporters calling it a classic test of precision and detractors scoffing at its lack of length. Only 113 yards from the Crows, or championship tees, it can play as short as 87 yards, neces-sitating a wedge or sand wedge over a gorge festooned with brambles to a perched green. No matter which camp you subscribe to, you still must hit a very accurate tee shot to be able to record a par.

The Links at Crowbush Cove is the jewel in Prince Edward Island's golfing crown. It has brought worldwide attention to the other excellent and affordable golf courses on the island such as Mill River, Brudenell, Green Gables and Belvedere. A new 18-hole, 7,300-yard course opened in late 1998 at Brudenell.

Crowbush Cove, the most notorious course in the province of Prince Edward Island, causes fits for just about everyone who plays here, especially if the wind is up. Barring extremely unusual conditions however (see main story), Crowbush Cove offers an enjoyable, reasonably priced round on a well-conditioned, links-style layout. Even PGA Tour stars such as Mark O'Meara and Fred Couples complimented the course when they played here in the 1998 Export 'A' Skins Game. They, along with John Daly and Canadian PGA Tour rookie Mike Weir, competed for $360,000. Although Weir led after day one with $45,000, Couples blew everyone away on day two, ending up with a total of $220,000. It was his fourth title in the event's six-year history. (Pictured: holes 12, 13, 14)

The closing hole at Mont Tremblant's Le Géant course is aptly named "Concentration." The 457-yard par 4 demands a superb tee shot followed by a mid-iron to a well-bunkered green. Play the back tees if you dare.

LE GÉANT AND LE DIABLE

Golf Courses

Public

Mont Tremblant was acquired in 1991 by Intrawest Corporation, a Vancouver-based company that is one of the foremost resort and real estate developers in North America, and the force behind the explosive growth of Whistler/Blackcomb in British Columbia. First opened in 1939, Mont Tremblant is the second-oldest ski resort on the continent. Located in the heart of the Laurentian Mountains of Quebec, the resort is within an easy drive of Montreal, Ottawa, Toronto, and New England.

Totaling 1,800 acres, the property presented an intriguing challenge to Intrawest to redevelop the aging infrastructure while building new condominiums, a conference centre, and other amenities, including 36 spectacular golf holes. At the time Intrawest purchased Mont Tremblant, a mediocre nine-hole course existed at the base of the ski hill. It did not fit with what Intrawest perceived as a world-class destination resort.

So, in 1993, based on a design by Thomas McBroom of

Le Géant Golf Course
Mont Tremblant, Quebec

	Length	Par
Double Black	6826	72
Black	6390	72
Blue	5959	72

Hole	Yards	Par		Hole	Yards	Par
1	510	4		10	159	5
2	429	4		11	311	4
3	173	5		12	547	3
4	406	4		13	329	4
5	385	5		14	380	5
6	174	3		15	393	3
7	578	4		16	202	4
8	492	4		17	495	4
9	406	3		18	457	4
OUT	3553	36		IN	3273	36
				Total	7056	72

Mont Tremblant: Even if you are brave enough to play from the back tees at the 457-yard 18th at Le Géant, you should stop at the blue tee box on your way to the fairway to admire one of the greatest views in golf. Trees form a dense backdrop to the green, a lake shimmers in the distance, and mountains, bedecked in ski runs, loom to your right. Then refocus your attention on playing the toughest par 4 on the course.

The tee shot on the par-4 11th pivots around a massive rock face about 200 yards out. The green on this 311-yarder is reachable from the tee if you carry the rocks.

Toronto, construction began on Le Géant, the first 18-hole championship course at Mont Tremblant. Opening in 1995, it led the way for Le Diable, a Michael Hurdzan/Dana Fry creation which opened in mid-1998.

The site at Mont Tremblant, although admittedly severe, provided both architectural firms with a plethora of possibilities: dramatic and varied topography, fabulous views of the nearby lake, river and mountains, and mature stands of both coniferous and deciduous trees. The result in both cases is a marvelous and distinctive sequence of holes.

At Le Géant, each hole has four sets of tees, stretching almost 6,900 yards from the very back — obviously for just the best players. The more forward tees provide an opportunity for golfers of lesser ability to enjoy their day. And that is the key to Le Géant: Play the appropriate tees. While McBroom emphasized playability, he was also constrained by the rugged terrain, meaning that errant shots are often penalized severely.

Respecting those natural constraints meant turning them into design features, so the course sits quite naturally on the land. The holes are laid out so each is in its own setting, winding through valleys at the base of the ski hill. Majestic rock outcroppings frame some of the fairways. On a few of Le Géant's holes, you are perched between the towering ski hill and the village below. Astoundingly, despite its 300-foot elevation change, not one hole plays uphill.

Le Géant's opening hole welcomes you with a generous fairway framed by stands of white pine, although cross-bunkers in front of the green will vex your approach. The second fairway is also wide open, although a lake running along the left perimeter may cause some

anxious moments. The par-3 third offers a tangible example of the character and theme of the golf course: The tees are on a broad rock outcrop with the green set far below in a wooded glade and protected by one narrow pot bunker. A distinctive and elegant golf hole.

Le Géant begins living up to its name on the par-4 fourth hole which runs parallel with the Devil's River and then plunges into ancient forest. Massive rock outcrops define the landing area, while the green is receptive to lofted or run-up approaches. The fifth hole is pure natural golf, from an elevated tee down through the woods to a generous landing area that slopes sharply to the right. The bunkerless green is backstopped by a massive granite face.

No. 6 may be the prettiest hole on Le Géant, a par 3 playing down from a rocky perch into a tiny green surrounded by forest. In contrast, the par-5 seventh plays

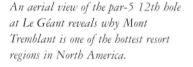

An aerial view of the par-5 12th hole at Le Géant reveals why Mont Tremblant is one of the hottest resort regions in North America.

almost 600 yards from the tips and defies even good golfers to get home in two, weaving through wildly heaving landscape to the distant green. At 461 yards, the eighth is the longest par 4 here, although long hitters will gain an advantage by hitting the downslope in the landing area. The front nine concludes with a narrow par 4 where it may be wise to leave the driver in the bag; how about a 3-wood followed by a 7-iron?

The back nine gets underway with a gorgeous par 3 of 158 yards from an elevated tee to a plateau green at the base of a granite wall. The 11th tests your concentration as you gasp at the stunning views. Once again, resist the driver. Fade a long iron to the corner of the dogleg instead. More great views greet you on the 12th tee, where you drive down into an alpine meadow framed by spruce, pine, and rock. The 13th and 14th are

both short but strategically challenging par 4s, preludes to the uncharacteristically benign 15th, which sits on the site of a former sand pit.

The finishing holes at Le Géant start with the 16th, a great par 3 which plays 202 yards from the championship tees. The par-5 17th is reachable with two perfect shots and the 18th hole has few peers in terms of drama and beauty. At 457 yards, it is the toughest of Le Géant's outstanding par 4s.

Le Diable is a fitting stablemate for Le Géant. It is set in a pine forest and features Arizona-style waste sand bunkers on 12 of its 18 holes. The other holes play high atop the mountain and offer spectacular vistas of Tremblant and the surrounding Laurentians. Only the very best will think to challenge Le Diable at its full length, an imposing 7,100 yards.

Le Géant is an engineering marvel. Despite the hundreds of feet of elevation changes on the course, not one hole plays uphill.

ROYAL MONTREAL

Golf Club

Architect: Dick Wilson
Head Professional: Bob Hogarth
Manager: Denzil Palmer
Superintendent: Ron Leishman

The early days of the history of golf in Canada are almost synonymous with the Royal Montreal Golf Club — the oldest golf club in North America, beating Royal Quebec onto the scene by a mere six months back in 1873. Royal Montreal's ground-breaking efforts didn't cease for decades. It was the first Canadian club to receive the "Royal" prefix (in 1884), the first in Canada to import an English golf professional (William Davis in 1881), the first on the continent to allow women members (1891), and it played host to the very first Canadian Open in 1904.

Now into its second century, the history of Royal Montreal is intertwined with that of the early settlement of this country. Golf had been played in the Montreal area by early fur traders, and a notice dating back 50 years prior to the founding of Royal Montreal invites members of the city's Scots community to a golf outing west of town. That the evolutionary process would continue to its inevitable outcome might not have been obvious in those days, although it is to those looking back.

The historic event came to pass on November 4, 1873, in the office of the Sidey Brothers, prominent Montreal businessmen. One of the founding members was Alexander Dennistoun, who served

as the first president and captain of Royal Montreal until 1890. The original site, called Fletcher's Field, was on the flank of Mount Royal and boasted six holes, which were probably sufficient for the 25 members. By 1895, the growth of both the city and the membership necessitated a move to the outskirts of Montreal.

Longtime members fondly recall this so-called "Dixie" site on the bank of the St. Lawrence River in what now is the westend suburb of Dorval. By 1922, this course featured 36 holes — the famed North and South layouts — designed by Willie Park Jr., architect of other fine Canadian layouts such as Weston Golf and Country Club and Calgary Golf and Country Club. The second of two clubhouses built on this location, and completed the same year as Park's courses, was widely acknowledged as the finest in Canada.

In 1957, Royal Montreal moved for the final time to a 650-acre site on a beautiful island called Ile Bizard northwest of Montreal. The club engaged Florida architect Dick Wilson, whose work on West Palm Beach Country Club in Florida and NCR Country Club in Ohio made him one of the most sought-after course designers of that era, to build two 18-hole courses at the new site. Wilson was suitably impressed by the club's choice of property. "The great feature of this place," he said, "is the great sweep of the landscape. That vista of the Lake of Two Mountains is the perfect backdrop to these courses."

Head Professional Bruce Murray knows the courses as well as anyone and admires the Wilson design. "A general feature of the Royal Montreal courses," he has said, "a tendency of Dick Wilson, is that the bunkering of all the holes is more apparent on the front of the green and the entrances are very narrow. The key is that bunkers are positioned very close to the putting surface, which makes Royal Montreal basically a second-shot layout. You've got to hit the ball up onto the green, so the premium is on accuracy."

Royal Montreal is often thought of as possessing only 18 holes — the renowned Blue course that played host to the Canadian Open in 1975 and 1980. Many golfers do not realize there are 27 other holes at Ile Bizard. "The Red course is just as good or better than the Blue," says Murray. "It may not be as spectacular because there is no water, but it is just as tight and testing. In many ways, it's similar to Scotland. The 13th and 14th holes, for example, have high mounds and well-bunkered greens. The fifth hole on the Red is an exceptional par-four — the Number 1 stroke hole. And Number 10 is a long, strong par-three with lots of sand and a narrow entrance to the green." As well, Murray points out that the so-called "Dixie" nine, which plays to 3,100 yards, is a collection of good holes that is often overlooked.

The Blue course is generally considered the tournament course. The group of the final four holes is acknowledged as one of the toughest

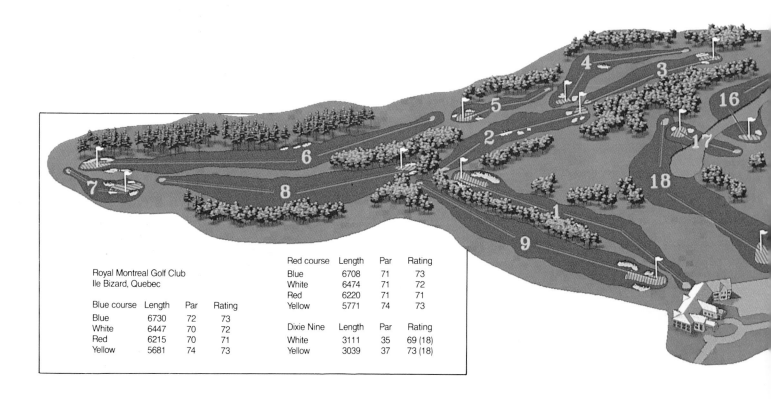

Royal Montreal Golf Club
Ile Bizard, Quebec

Blue course	Length	Par	Rating
Blue	6730	72	73
White	6447	70	72
Red	6215	70	71
Yellow	5681	74	73

Red course	Length	Par	Rating
Blue	6708	71	73
White	6474	71	72
Red	6220	71	71
Yellow	5771	74	73

Dixie Nine	Length	Par	Rating
White	3111	35	69 (18)
Yellow	3039	37	73 (18)

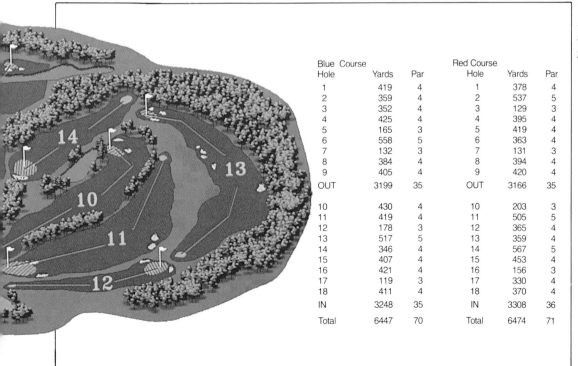

The 16th hole on Royal Montreal's Blue Course has been called one of the best par-fours in the country.

Blue Course			Red Course		
Hole	Yards	Par	Hole	Yards	Par
1	419	4	1	378	4
2	359	4	2	537	5
3	352	4	3	129	3
4	425	4	4	395	4
5	165	3	5	419	4
6	558	5	6	363	4
7	132	3	7	131	3
8	384	4	8	394	4
9	405	4	9	420	4
OUT	3199	35	OUT	3166	35
10	430	4	10	203	3
11	419	4	11	505	5
12	178	3	12	365	4
13	517	5	13	359	4
14	346	4	14	567	5
15	407	4	15	453	4
16	421	4	16	156	3
17	119	3	17	330	4
18	411	4	18	370	4
IN	3248	35	IN	3308	36
Total	6447	70	Total	6474	71

tests in Canada. Number 15, a 400-yard par-four with the wind generally following, may dictate a fairway wood off the tee, for a well-struck drive could end up in the lake. Hit a seven- or eight-iron over the water but make sure you take enough club to get to the green. The reason? Royal Montreal's greens feature narrow throats with heavy frontal bunkering. "You can hit to the middle or back of the greens here all day," says Murray, "and not get into trouble. Just don't be short, otherwise you'll have little puff shots over bunkers on every hole and those can wear you out in a hurry."

The 16th is "as good a par-four as there is in Canada," says Murray. The lake runs the length of the left side, so the better player will try to cut the ball in over the lake to the centre of the fairway. He still faces a four- or five-iron uphill and over a pond. Number 17 is a great par-three: caught between the water and a large bunker left is a small green that narrows severely at the entrance. Only a short-iron effort at 120 yards, this hole can wreak psychological and physical damage.

The finishing hole is a splendid par-four with an interesting tournament history. Jack Nicklaus, with a one-shot lead over Tom Weiskopf in the 1975 Open, splashed his one-iron effort into water at the corner of the dogleg. Although his heroic third shot (after taking a penalty) reached the green and he salvaged a bogey, Weiskopf made par to force the playoff which Nicklaus lost.

The Red Course at Royal Mont-real: the par-three 10th hole requires length and accuracy.

The short 17th on the Blue Course severely punishes an errant tee shot.

Charlie Murray

History, of Course

Another Royal Montreal claim to fame is that only five head professionals, three of them with the surname Murray, have been employed here in 110 years.

Willie Davis was brought to the original site in 1881. (Recent research indicates it may have been Davis, not Willie Dunn, who designed historic Shinnecock Hills in the United States after he left Royal Montreal.) The others were Charlie Murray, a two-time Canadian Open champion, and his son Kenny.

The present head professional, Bruce Murray (no relation to Charley and Kenny), took over after Pat Fletcher, remembered as the last Canadian to win our national championship in 1954. But Jack Young holds the individual record: he served as an assistant professional here for more than 50 years!

PHOTOGRAPHIC CREDITS

Unless otherwise noted, all photographs in this book are by Michael French. Doug Ball, 142–147; Bell Bay, 100–105; Capilano Golf Club, 51; Crowbush Cove, 220–225; Le Géant and Le Diable 226–231; Dieter Hessell, 166, 171; Highland Links, 106, 110; Royal Montreal Golf Club, 237; Score Magazine, 15; Don Vickery, 183.